Best Easy Day Hikes Series

Best Easy Day Hikes
Madison

W9-AEB-871

Johnny Molloy

FALCONGUIDES

GUILFORD, CONNECTICUT
HELENA, MONTANA

AN IMPRINT OF GLOBE PEQUOT PRESS

To buy books in quantity for corporate use
or incentives, call **(800) 962-0973**
or e-mail **premiums@GlobePequot.com**.

FALCONGUIDES®

FalconGuides is an imprint of Globe Pequot Press.
Falcon, FalconGuides, and Outfit Your Mind are registered trademarks
of Morris Book Publishing, LLC.

Maps: Daniel Lloyd © Morris Book Publishing LLC
Project editor: Julie Marsh
Layout: Mary Ballachino

Library of Congress Cataloging-in-Publication Data is available on file.
ISBN 978-0-7627-9018-0

Printed in the United States of America

10 9 8 7 6 5 4 3 2 1

Contents

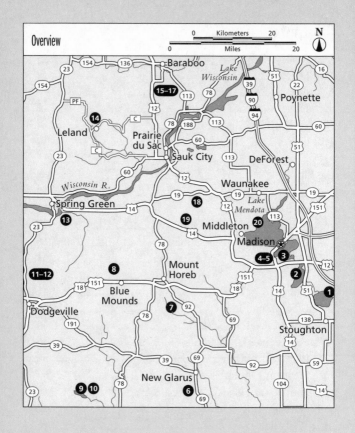

Map Legend

═══(94)═══	Interstate Highway
═══(14)═══	US Highway
═══(19)═══	State Highway
───────	Local/County Road
= = = = = =	Unpaved Road
┼─┼─┼─┼─┼	Railroad
▬▬▬▬▬▬	Featured Trail
─ ─ ─ ─ ─ ─	Trail
───────	Paved Trail
～～～	River/Creek
⬭	Body of Water
～	Marsh
▭	Local/State Park
▭	National Park
⛵	Boat Launch
▭	Bench
⌣	Bridge
▲	Campground
⊛	Capital
•─•	Gate
❓	Information Center
🅿	Parking
🛆	Picnic Area
■	Point of Interest/Trailhead
🚻	Restrooms
○	Town
⓫	Trailhead
🔭	Viewpoint/Overlook
≋	Waterfall

Acknowledgments

Thanks to all the people who helped me with this book, primarily Keri Anne Molloy for all her companionship on the trail, for driving, and for other trail work. Thanks to the people at FalconGuides, especially Katie Benoit. Thanks to DeLorme for their accurate Global Positioning Systems and to Sierra Designs for quality tents and outdoor clothing. In addition, thanks to all the park personnel who answered my incessant questions while trying to manage these jewels of greater Madison. The biggest thanks go to the local southern Wisconsin hikers and trail builders, as well as those who visit this scenic slice of America, for without y'all, there would not be trails in the first place.

Introduction

The astonishing view stretched out beyond the bluff and water. I stood on the sandstone outcrop. Hundreds of feet below lay Devils Lake, a Southern Wisconsin icon. East Bluff, with its rock cliffs and massive boulder gardens, stretched in the distance. Forested lowlands extended to the yon. West Bluff was but one of many scenic and rewarding destinations in this guide and encapsulated this marvelous parcel of greater Madison. I mentally reflected on other destinations, recounting all the worthwhile hikes in the area. To the south the trails along Lake Waubesa at Lake Farm Park displayed another destination where hikers could walk a scenic shoreline. The University of Wisconsin Arboretum, near Lake Wingra, presented pathways skirting past Indian effigy mounds and amid several forest types and around the famed Curtis Prairie, site of the world's first prairie restoration project. Turville Point Conservation Park was yet another in-town hike. Here, trail trekkers could walk through an oak savanna and gain a lakeside view of the Madison skyline, highlighted by the Wisconsin state capitol.

Rolling woods and big trees characterized the hike at New Glarus Woods State Park. Fast-moving Deer Creek at Donald Park provided contrast with the lakes on other hikes. The views from the top of Blue Mound still echo in my memory. The prairie hikes at Lake Kegonsa and Governor Nelson State Parks allowed me to fully explore the all-important prairie ecosystem. Yellowstone Lake State Park had its own oak groves, savannas, prairies, and lake views. Of course, Governor Dodge State Park had its two lakes about which to brag. The hike along Pine Cliff was a menagerie of stone and evergreen. The hike to Stephens Falls stands out for its historic as well as natural history. The cataract tumbles over a stone face into a wooded glen. The stream then pours through a geological wonder of a canyon. I saw the canyon from the bottom and the top from stone bluffs. The hike was topped off with a visit to a homesite, complete with interpretive information.

Speaking of history, how could I forget the hike to the shot tower atop bluffs overlooking the Wisconsin River? The views extended to the distant horizon and the labor obviously involved in digging the shot shaft was hard to comprehend. The past came alive at Natural Bridge State Park, where aboriginal Wisconsonians sheltered near the largest natural arch in the state. The greater Madison landscape was affected in other ways, namely the glaciers that scraped much of the state. A pair of hikes on the Ice Age Trail at Indian Lake Park and near Table Bluff showcased still other fascinating landscapes through which to hike. And it all came back to the panoramas from the bluffs ringing Devils Lake. I considered the fine views, extensive history, and variety of hikes around Madison and concluded that the greater capital area is truly a fine place to hike.

With this book in hand and willing feet, you can explore southern Wisconsin. No matter where you go, the trails in this book will enhance your outdoor experience and leave you appreciating the natural splendors of greater Madison. Enjoy.

The Nature of Madison

Greater Madison's hiking grounds range from singletrack wooded paths along lakes and hills to well-marked nature trails to strolls on interpretive paths. Hikes in this guide cover the gamut. While by definition a "best easy day hike" is not strenuous and generally poses little danger to the traveler, knowing a few details about the nature of southern Wisconsin will enhance your explorations.

Weather
Southern Wisconsin certainly experiences all four seasons. Summer can be warm, with sporadic hot spells. Morning hikers can avoid any heat and the common afternoon thunderstorms. Hiking becomes more comfortable when the first northerly fronts of fall sweep cool clear air across the Badger State. Crisp mornings give way to warm afternoons. Fall is drier than summer. Winter will bring frigid subfreezing days, chilling rains, and significant snow. However, a brisk hiking pace will keep you warm. Each cold month has a few days of somewhat mild weather. Make the most of them. Spring will be more variable. A warm day can be followed by a cold, snowy one. Spring rains bring regrowth but also keep hikers indoors. However, any avid hiker will find more good hiking days than they will have time to hike in spring and every other season.

Critters
Greater Madison trail treaders will encounter mostly benign creatures on these trails, such as deer, squirrels, wild turkeys, a variety of songbirds, and rabbits. More rarely seen (during the daylight hours especially) are coyotes and raccoons. Deer in some of the parks are remarkably tame and may linger on or close to the trail as you approach. If you feel uncomfortable when encountering any critter, keep your distance and they will generally keep theirs.

Be Prepared

Hiking around greater Madison is generally safe. Still, hikers should be prepared, whether they are out for a short stroll at the UW Arboretum or venturing into Natural Bridge State Park. Some specific advice:

- Know the basics of first aid, including how to treat bleeding, bites and stings, and fractures, strains, or sprains. Pack a first-aid kit on every excursion.

- Familiarize yourself with the symptoms of heat exhaustion and heatstroke. Heat exhaustion symptoms include heavy sweating, muscle cramps, headache, dizziness, and fainting. Should you or any of your hiking party exhibit any of these symptoms, cool the victim down immediately by rehydrating and getting him or her to an air-conditioned location. Cold showers also help reduce body temperature. Heatstroke is much more serious: The victim may lose consciousness and the skin is hot and dry to the touch. In this event call 911 immediately.

- Regardless of the weather, your body needs a lot of water while hiking. A full 32-ounce bottle is the minimum for these short hikes, but more is always better. Bring a full water bottle, whether water is available along the trail or not.

- Don't drink from streams, rivers, creeks, or lakes without treating or filtering the water first. Waterways and water bodies may host a variety of contaminants, including giardia, which can cause serious intestinal unrest.

- Prepare for extremes of both heat and cold by dressing in layers.

- Carry a backpack in which you can store extra clothing, ample drinking water and food, and whatever goodies, like guidebooks, cameras, and binoculars, you might want. Consider bringing a GPS with tracking capabilities or enable the GPS function on your phone.

- Cell phone coverage is generally good, but you can never be absolutely sure until you are on location. In downtown Madison you are virtually assured of coverage, but the hinterlands may be another story. Bring your device, but make sure you've turned it off or got it on the vibrate setting while hiking. Nothing like a "wake the dead"-loud ring to startle every creature on the trail, including fellow hikers.

- Keep children under careful watch. Trails travel along cliffs and beside lakes and streams, most of which are not recommended for swimming. Be watchful along designated overlooks. Hazards along some of the trails include poison ivy, uneven footing, and steep drop-offs; make sure children do not stray from the designated route. Children should carry a plastic whistle; if they become lost, they should stay in one place and blow the whistle to summon help.

Leave No Trace

Trails in southern Wisconsin are well used during spring, summer, and fall—the hiking season. Many trails are closed to hikers when snow is on the ground. As trail users, we must be especially vigilant to make sure our passage leaves no lasting mark. Here are some basic guidelines for preserving trails in the region:

- Pack out all your own trash, including biodegradable items like orange peels. You might also pack out garbage left by less considerate hikers.

- Don't approach or feed any wild creatures—the ground squirrel eyeing your snack food is best able to survive if it remains self-reliant.

- Don't pick wildflowers or gather rocks, antlers, feathers, or other treasures along the trail, especially historic relics. Removing these items will only take away from the next hiker's experience and steal a piece of the historic puzzle found in area parks.

- Avoid damaging trailside soils and prairie plants by remaining on the established route. This is also a good rule of thumb for avoiding poison ivy and other common regional trailside irritants.

- Be courteous by not making loud noises while hiking.

- Some of these trails are multiuse, which means you'll share them with other hikers, trail runners, mountain bikers, and equestrians. Familiarize yourself with the proper trail etiquette, yielding the trail when appropriate.

- Use outhouses at trailheads or along the trail.

For more information visit LNT.org.

Madison Area Boundaries and Corridors

For the purposes of this guide, the best easy day hikes are confined to a 1-hour drive from Madison, Wisconsin.

Two major interstates and a major highway converge around the capital. Directions to trailheads are given from these interstates and other arteries. They include I-90/94, I-39/90, and US 12/US 18—commonly known as the Beltline.

Land Management

The following government organizations manage most of the public lands described in this guide and can provide further information on these hikes and other trails in their service areas.

- Wisconsin State Parks, 101 S. Webster St., PO Box 7921, Madison, WI 53707; (608) 266-2621; www.dnr.wi.gov
- Dane County Parks, 1 Fen Oak Ct., Madison, WI 53718; (608) 242-4576; www.countyofdane.com
- City of Madison Parks, City-County Building, Suite 104, 210 Martin Luther King Jr. Blvd., Madison, WI 53703; (608) 266-4711; www.cityofmadison.com/parks

How to Use This Guide

This guide is designed to be simple and easy to use. Each hike is described with a map and summary information that delivers the trail's vital statistics including length, difficulty, fees and permits, park hours, canine compatibility, and trail contacts. Directions to the trailhead are also provided, along with a general description of what you'll see along the way. A detailed route finder (Miles and Directions) sets forth mileages between significant landmarks along the trail.

Hike Selection

This guide describes trails that are accessible to every hiker, whether visiting from out of town or someone lucky enough to live in the capital area. The hikes are no longer than 4.4 miles round-trip, and most are considerably shorter. They range in difficulty from flat excursions perfect for a family outing to more challenging hilly treks. While these trails are among the best, keep in mind that nearby trails, often in the same park or preserve, may offer options better suited to your needs. I've sought to space hikes throughout the greater Madison region, so wherever your starting point, you'll find a great easy day hike nearby.

Difficulty Ratings

These are all easy hikes, but easy is a relative term. To aid in the selection of a hike that suits particular needs and abilities, each is rated easy, moderate, or more challenging. Bear in mind that even challenging routes can be made easy by hiking within your limits and taking rests when you need them.

- Easy hikes are generally short and flat, taking no longer than an hour to complete.
- Moderate hikes involve increased distance and relatively mild changes in elevation and will take 1 to 2 hours to complete.
- More challenging hikes feature some steep stretches and greater distances and generally take longer than 2 hours to complete.

These are completely subjective ratings—consider that what you think is easy is entirely dependent on your level of fitness and the adequacy of your gear (primarily shoes). If you are hiking with a group, you should select a hike with a rating that is appropriate for the least fit and prepared in your party.

Approximate hiking times are based on the assumption that on flat ground, most walkers average 2 miles per hour. Adjust that rate by the steepness of the terrain and your level of fitness (subtract time if you are an aerobic animal and add time if you are hiking with kids), and you have a ballpark hiking duration. Be sure to add more time if you plan to picnic or take part in other activities like bird watching or photography.

Trail Finder

Best Hikes for Lake Lovers

Best Hikes for Children

Best Hikes for Dogs

Best Hikes for Great Views

Best Hikes for Solitude

Best Hikes for History Buffs

Best Hikes for Nature Lovers

1 Lake Kegonsa Loop

Set on the northeast shore of Lake Kegonsa in the state park of the same name, this hike first traces an interpretive trail through forest, where you can learn more about Southern Wisconsin's plant heritage. From there the hike breaks out into restored prairie, where more floral vestiges of the Badger State shine. The easy-to-reach state park makes for a well-maintained and scenic setting, and the trails are mostly level. Other pastimes at Lake Kegonsa, such as swimming, camping, boating, and fishing, are a breeze to integrate into your trip here.

Distance: 2.4-mile double loop
Hiking time: About 1 to 2 hours
Difficulty: Easy
Trail surface: Natural surfaces, fine gravel
Best season: When snow is not on the ground
Other trail users: Skiers when snow is on the ground
Canine compatibility: Dogs not permitted

Fees and permits: Parking pass required
Schedule: 6 a.m. to 11 p.m. daily
Maps: *Lake Kegonsa State Park; USGS Stoughton*
Trail contacts: Lake Kegonsa State Park, 2405 Door Creek Rd., Stoughton, WI 53589; (608) 873-9695; www.dnr.wi.gov

Finding the trailhead: From exit 147 on I-39/94, take County Road N south a short distance to Koskonong Road. Turn right and follow Koskonong Road for 1.7 miles to Door Creek Road. Turn left on Door Creek Road and follow it 0.9 mile to the park entrance on your right. Pass the entrance station and turn right toward the park campground. Drive a short distance and the trailhead is located on your left, near the restrooms. GPS: N42 58.8178' / W89 14.1760'

The Hike

Some of Southern Wisconsin's natural beauty spots are hard to reach, requiring long, winding drives through farms and fields on two-lane roads. Back in 1961 the state recognized two things: Wisconsin needed more natural preserves within easy reach of the populace, and the American interstate system was to play a large role in the future of auto travel. With that in mind, the state set about creating state parks near interstates. Thus, Lake Kegonsa State Park came to be. Now, Madisonians can easily reach this state park via I-39/94.

Lake Kegonsa is the southernmost of Madison's glacially created Four Lakes, the most notable being Lake Mendota, beside which Madison rises, followed by Lake Monona, Lake Waubesa, and finally Lake Kegonsa. The Yahara River strings together these four aquatic pearls of Southern Wisconsin.

And there is reason to visit Lake Kegonsa State Park in addition to the trails. After five decades of steady work, improving the natural habitat as well as visitor facilities, the state park has received another major overhaul. A new visitor center/entrance station was built, the park swim beach and boat ramps were relocated and improved, and large picnic areas were established. Expect visitor facilities to further improve, including the addition of more trails.

Even the pathways on this hike have received work. The second loop of this trek—the Prairie Trail—was made accessible for all. It was fairly level to begin with, but the addition of packed gravel allow trail enthusiasts who use wheelchairs to grab a view of tawny waving grasses, see the kaleidoscope of swaying wildflowers soaking in the summer sun, and perhaps spot a deer at the edge of the field and forest.

The first part of the hike traces the White Oak Nature Trail, an interpretive path with signage to help you more easily identify the trees of Southern Wisconsin, thereby impressing your friends on your next day hike. The trail is gently rolling but sans serious vertical variation. Feel like exploring more? The state park also has the half-mile Lakeshore Trail, the half-mile Oak Knoll Trail, and the short Bluebird Trail.

The quality wooded campground, with many fine private sites, is located near the Prairie Trail and White Oak Nature Trail. However, most of the park action is astride Lake Kegonsa. Multiple fishing piers allow boatless anglers to vie for northern pike, walleye, and panfish. Many visitors launch their boats to ply 3,200-acre Lake Kegonsa for fishing and boating pleasure. The swim beach is a huge summertime draw. Speaking of seasons, during winter, when snow is on the ground, Lake Kegonsa State Park trails are closed to hikers and open to cross-country skiers.

Miles and Directions

0.0 From the trailhead parking area, with the restrooms to your right and a volleyball court on your left, look right for the White Oak Nature Trail. Enter the woods on a wide double-track path and stay right again, looping the trail counterclockwise. White oaks, shagbark hickory, and walnut trees shade the path.

0.3 Cruise behind the state park campground, off to your right. User-created spur trails link the trail and campsites.

0.4 Begin curving west, as the trail turns west into an oak savanna, with a wider dispersal of trees.

0.5 Pass some Indian Mounds, part of the mound builders, whose effigy mounds are found near many of the Madison-area lakes.

0.8 Pass near a pine plantation to your right.

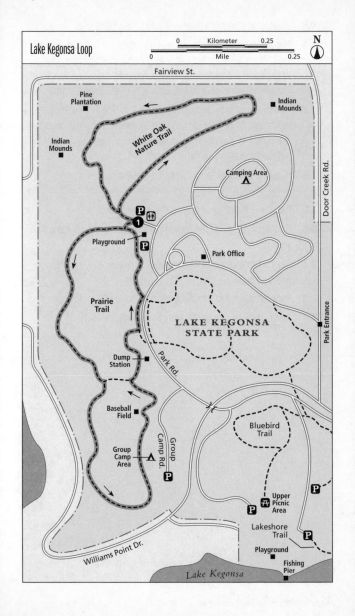

Lake Kegonsa Loop

Fairview St.

Pine Plantation

Indian Mounds

Indian Mounds

White Oak Nature Trail

Camping Area

Door Creek Rd.

P **1**

Playground

P

Park Office

Prairie Trail

LAKE KEGONSA STATE PARK

Park Entrance

Dump Station

Park Rd.

Baseball Field

Group Camp Area

Group Camp Rd.

P

Bluebird Trail

P

Upper Picnic Area

P

Lakeshore Trail

Playground

Fishing Pier

Williams Point Dr.

Lake Kegonsa

N

0   Kilometer   0.25

0   Mile   0.25

0.9 Pass near another effigy mound to your right.

1.1 Return to the trailhead. Here, turn right and join the Prairie Trail. Pass a group fire ring used for park interpretive talks. Enter open grassland, roughly paralleling the transition zone between prairie and forest, on a gravel all-access path.

1.5 Reach a trail intersection. A shortcut on the Prairie Trail leads left. Stay right on the Oak Savanna Trail. Hike along the nexus of prairie and woodland. Enjoy sweeping views across the open prairie.

1.8 Bisect a grove of locust trees as the Prairie Trail curves north. Walk near the group camp.

1.9 Pass an official spur trail to the group camp.

2.0 Stay straight as a trail leaves right across the park road to your right.

2.1 Reach the other end of the shortcut across the Prairie Trail. Keep straight.

2.2 Pass another trail crossing the park road. Keep straight.

2.4 Arrive back at the trailhead, completing the loop.

2 Lake Farm County Park

This hike visits the shores of Lake Waubesa, one of the major lakes in the immediate Madison region. Since Lake Farm County Park borders Lake Waubesa, it presents an opportunity to walk along the water's edge for a fair distance. Leave a fine picnic area, then head for Lake Waubesa. After reaching the shore, cruise both waterside and on elevated hills above the lake, where far-reaching views await. The hike then passes through a restored prairie and finally along wetlands and ponds that provide an additional aquatic experience.

Distance: 2.2-mile loop
Hiking time: About 1.5 to 2 hours
Difficulty: Easy to moderate
Trail surface: Natural surfaces
Best season: When snow is not on the ground
Other trail users: Skiers when snow is on the ground
Canine compatibility: Leashed dogs allowed with county dog permit

Fees and permits: None
Schedule: Dawn to dusk daily
Maps: *Lake Farm Park; USGS Madison East*
Trail contacts: Lake Farm Park, 4330 Libby Rd., Madison, WI 53711; (608) 224-3730; www.countyofdane.com

Finding the trailhead: From exit 264 on US 12/18, the Madison Beltline, take South Town Drive for 0.8 mile to Moorland (along the way, South Town Drive becomes Raewood). Turn left on Moorland and follow it 0.8 mile to Libby Road. Turn left on Libby Road and follow it 0.5 mile to enter Lake Farm Park on your left. Park at Shelter #1, shortly after entering the park, on your right. GPS: N43 1.594' / W89 19.950'

The Hike

Waterfront property on one of greater Madison's big four lakes—Lake Mendota, Lake Monona, Lake Waubesa, and Lake Kegonsa—can go for big bucks if and when it comes up for sale. A large undeveloped tract of waterfront property is still rarer in the fast-growing capital area. Lake Farm Park, however, is such a parcel. Managed by Dane County, the park, situated on the western shore of Lake Waubesa, covers 2,074 acres and presents multiple recreation opportunities in addition to hiking. Boating, fishing, camping, and bicycling are popular here, as is picnicking. In addition, the park is linked to the Capital City Trail.

The park has potential for wildlife observation. I have personally seen deer, bald eagles, and songbirds galore while hiking here. In addition to this hike, Lake Farm Park has a wildlife observation deck and boardwalk that leads to lagoons where waterfowl congregate in season.

The hike traces doubletrack grass paths that lace Lake Farm Park. The trails are mostly level, with just a little vertical variation along the shore of Lake Waubesa. Though not all the trail intersections are signed, a trail map and a modicum of map-reading skills will get you through the trail system.

Picnic Shelter #1 makes for a good jumping-off spot. It offers shaded dining, restrooms, and ample parking. You quickly enter woods, passing a small pond on your left before starting the loop portion of the hike. The circuit first leads to the park boat launch, which can be crowded in the morning and on weekends. A partly shaded path then travels north along the banks of Lake Waubesa. The path rollercoasters along the sloped shoreline, sometimes eye-level with the water, sometimes elevated above the tarn. Pass near a pair of picnic shelters.

After a rewarding shoreline trek, the path skirts the park's group camp before entering prairie. Like many other southern Wisconsin parks, the meadow is under restoration. Additional mown paths may prove slightly confusing, but the primary route is obvious.

Your return route takes the group-camp access road to reach another grassy doubletrack. It wanders under soaring trees astride a series of ponds and wetlands that present wildlife-viewing opportunities. All too soon, you are back at the trailhead, ready to engage in other outdoor pursuits available at Lake Farm County Park. *Note:* The trails here are closed to hikers when snow is on the ground, at which time they are open only to cross-country skiers.

Miles and Directions

0.0 From the Picnic Shelter #1 parking area, walk under an archway by a silo/observation tower on a grassy trail, eastbound. Immediately reach a trail split. The route going left heads a short distance to a pond. Stay right.

0.1 Reach the loop portion of the hike. Stay right here on a doubletrack, heading south under tall cottonwoods and walnut trees. The trail soon turns northeast.

0.2 Come to the boat ramp parking area. Walk toward the boat ramp and you will see a small dock to the left of the ramp. Head to the dock, then look for a grassy track leading north along the edge of Lake Waubesa. Picturesque overhanging oaks line the path.

0.4 The trail travels near Picnic Shelter #2 to your left and a fishing pier to your right. Keep north along the shore of Lake Waubesa.

0.6 Pass Picnic Shelter #3 on your left.

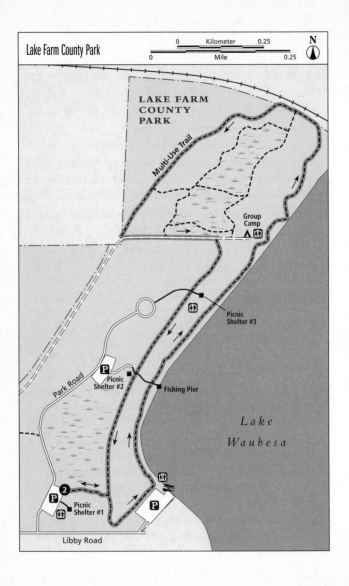

Lake Farm County Park

LAKE FARM
COUNTY
PARK

Multi-Use Trail

Group
Camp

Picnic
Shelter #3

Park Road

P

Picnic
Shelter #2

Fishing Pier

Lake

Waubesa

2

P

Picnic
Shelter #1

P

Libby Road

0   Kilometer   0.25
0   Mile   0.25

N

0.8 Skirt the edge of the group camp. Drop to the right, back along the shore of Lake Waubesa. The path works off and on the hill rising from the lakeshore.

1.0 Reach the northern end of the park, bordered by a railroad track. Turn northeast then southwesterly, passing spurs leading left across the prairie. Keep southwest, entering a mix of woods.

1.5 Meet the road leading left to the group camp. Turn left here, heading due east on the group camp access road. Pass prairieland to your left.

1.7 Leave right on a grassy trail just before reaching the group camp. Head southwest under tall cottonwoods.

1.8 Pass Picnic Shelter #3 again.

2.0 Pass behind Picnic Shelter #2. View an alluring pond bordered with willows. Look for wildlife here. More ponds lie ahead.

2.1 Complete the loop portion of the hike. Turn right toward Picnic Shelter #1.

2.2 Arrive back at the trailhead, completing the hike.

3 Turville Point Conservation Park

Enjoy this quick-access, in-town hike on the shores of Lake Monona. The natural preserve is adjacent to Olin Park, which offers traditional park facilities. This hike explores a hilly shoreline cloaked in oak savanna and prairie. After rolling through hardwood-studded hills, you will arrive at Lake Monona. Enjoy walking along the shoreline. The steepness of the hills here will surprise you. Grab a view of the Wisconsin capital skyline from Turville Point. Leave the lake and wander through more hills before arriving at the trailhead.

Distance: 1.4-mile loop
Hiking time: About 1 to 1.5 hours
Difficulty: Easy
Trail surface: Natural surfaces
Best season: Year-round
Other trail users: None
Canine compatibility: Leashed dogs permitted
Fees and permits: None

Schedule: 4 a.m. to dusk daily
Maps: *Turville Point Conservation Park; USGS Madison West, Madison East*
Trail contacts: Turville Point Conservation Park, City of Madison Parks Division, PO Box 2987, Madison, WI 53701; (608) 266-4711; www.cityofmadison .com/parks/

Finding the trailhead: From the Madison Beltline, US 12/18, take exit 263, John Nolen Drive. Follow John Nolen Drive north 0.7 mile to a traffic light, with Olin Avenue on the left and Olin Turville Court on your right. Turn right on Olin Turville Court, cross the railroad tracks, and immediately turn right into a large parking lot on your right. At the far end of the parking lot, you will see a sign that reads TURVILLE POINT fronting the woods. The hike starts here. GPS: N43 3.121' / W89 22.584'

The Hike

Turville Point Conservation Park and its twin, Olin Park, are situated on the shore of Lake Monona. They have a rich history. Together comprising a little over 100 acres, they were oak forest and wild prairie before being cleared as a farm by Henry Turville, an Englishman who settled in Madison in the mid-1800s. Of course, back in those days Turville Point was out in the country. It was not long after Turville started his farm in 1854 that he sold off part of the property. It became a sanatorium called the Water Cure. Soon this quackery-based healing joint closed down. However, after the Civil War the property became a resort where Southerners could escape the summer heat. A hotel was built on the shoreline. After a decade the resort burned down. The property was then rented by a Christian organization that held summer revivals there. After simply putting up tents during the summer season, they eventually built a large wooden pavilion along with a few other buildings. The land became the property of the Wisconsin Sunday School Assembly, which prospered for years. Next door the Turville Farm continued through successive generations, changing their emphasis from vegetables to flowers.

In the 1960s the city of Madison used eminent domain to force the sale of the Turville Farm for a business development. However, the development deal never came to be, and the city kept the property anyway. The land was mostly neglected during this time. Finally, in 1995 the old farm was declared a conservation park. Since then, what is sometimes referred to as Turville Woods has been managed to improve the native vegetation while burning and cutting invasive plants. They have even established a prairie in the center of the 64-acre plot. The prairie is at the highest, most level part of Turville Point Conservation Park and was the primary farming zone when the land was used for agriculture.

Today, a set of intertwined trails, used by hikers during the warm season and skiers when there's snow, runs throughout the property. This particular hike follows the outermost loop of the web of trails. You will stay primarily in woods, but much of the short walk is along or near the shoreline of Lake Monona. Grab some views of the lake, from water level as well as from a high hill. The best view comes from Turville Point, where the Madison skyline stands across Lake Monona. After a few hikes here, you will know the trail system. The intersections are not signed. However, in a 64-acre plot bordered by a lake, a railroad track, and another small park, how long can you stay lost?

If you are into more traditional park activities, Olin Park adjoins Turville Point Conservation Park. Olin Park has a boat launch, swimming beach, picnic pavilion, picnic area, and restroom as well as ball fields. And since these two parks join each other, it is essentially their management that makes them different entities.

Miles and Directions

0.0 From the trailhead parking area, with your back to Turville Court, walk a few feet, entering woods on a concrete track. Then head right (southbound) on a natural-surface path, passing through oak, pine, and cherry trees.

0.1 Stay right at two successive intersections. Turn east, running parallel to the railroad tracks. Look for blackened tree trunks, signs of prescribed fire.

0.5 Reach Lake Monona. Turn left (north) and begin to gain aquatic vistas in clearings between trees.

0.6 Climb a steep hill well above the shoreline on a singletrack path. Note the adjacent restored oak savanna.

Turville Point Conservation Park

Lake Monona

Pavilion

OLIN PARK

P

Prairie

Turville Point
Conservation
Park Trail

Turville Bay

Olin-Turville Ct.

W. Olin Ave.

John Nolen Dr.

12 18

0.7 A trail comes in on your left. Keep parallel to the lake, then descend.

0.8 Come back along the shore.

0.9 Arrive at Turville Point. Stop and soak in views of the Madison skyline, with the state capitol clearly visible across the shore. Curve away from the point, but run roughly parallel to the shore.

1.2 Pass a spur trail leading to the pavilion at Olin Park next door. Turn south.

1.3 Come to an old concrete drive. Here, a spur trail leads left to the park prairie. Stay straight on the concrete drive.

1.4 Reach the trailhead and the end of this hike.

4 UW Arboretum Big Spring Hike

This hike explores the northern parcel of the University of Wisconsin Arboretum, near Lake Wingra. Leave the hiker trailhead, then explore some Indian effigy mounds. After that, take off in hilly woods, dropping to visit Big Spring and wetlands along the south shore of Lake Wingra. Next, head into the forest of Gallistel Woods and the Lost City Forest. Visit Teal Pond, a watery wetland with a boardwalk. Just for contrast, the final part of the hike bisects Longenecker Gardens, where trees are planted by species and type.

Distance: 2.7-mile loop

Hiking time: About 2 to 2.5 hours

Difficulty: Moderate

Trail surface: Natural surfaces

Best season: Year-round

Other trail users: None

Canine compatibility: Dogs not permitted

Fees and permits: None

Schedule: 7 a.m. to 10 p.m. daily

Maps: *UW Arboretum; USGS Madison West*

Trail contacts: University of Wisconsin Arboretum, 1207 Seminole Hwy., Madison, WI 53711; (608) 263-7888; www.uwarboretum.org

Finding the trailhead: From exit 260 on the Madison Beltline, US 12/18, take Fish Hatchery Road north for 1.1 miles to Wingra Drive. Turn left on Wingra Drive and follow it 0.6 mile to Arboretum Drive. Turn left on Arboretum Drive and follow it 1.7 miles to the Wingra Woods trailhead on your right, 0.5 mile before reaching the arboretum visitor center. GPS: N43 2.753' / W89 25.643'

The Hike

Madison residents are fortunate to have the University of Wisconsin Arboretum within their midst. More than simply a collection of trees, the arboretum is a pioneer of ecological restoration—returning land to its natural condition with native species after it has been inhabited by or adversely affected by settlement. It is also a place where traditional gardens, as well as plant and tree collections from Wisconsin and around the world, can be enjoyed. It started back in the 1930s when Madison was growing rapidly and city residents saw the need for green space. The city began purchasing land for parks. Since the Great Depression was in full swing, land was cheap. Then along came the Civilian Conservation Corps (CCC), a government work project that employed hundreds of young men. They were stationed at the arboretum for six years, doing a lot of the grunt work and changing the affected landscape, mostly fields and pastures, into an arboretum.

Over the decades, the arboretum has expanded to 1,200 acres, stretching south from Lake Wingra. The University of Wisconsin has been deeply involved in the arboretum from its beginning. Today the arboretum is important for students and teachers doing research on the ecosystem contained within its boundaries.

The arboretum is divided into named sections, either based on the ecosystem within a tract or a name associated with the tract of land. The arboretum has expanded over the years with additional parcels added over time. This particular hike starts in the Wingra Woods. Here, make a small loop around a series of effigy mounds, similar to others in the greater Madison area. The hike then circles through Wingra

Woods, under the shadows of a classic northern hardwood forest. Yellow birch, beech, and sugar maple, along with hemlock trees, grow on a north-facing slope descending to Lake Wingra. Stop and visit Big Spring, a rocked-in upwelling of water. The hike then joins a boardwalk and traverses a wetland and stream that feeds Lake Wingra.

From here the trek heads south into Gallistel Woods, another northern hardwood haven. Cruise through the low-lying Lost City Forest. Once slated to become a subdivision, the already-platted land was too wet and land values dropped as it was being showcased, so the development instead became part of the arboretum.

The hike then passes by more wetlands, including the Teal Pond, which you'll be able to view. Finally, the trail visits Longenecker Gardens. With more than 2,000 plants on display, it is a classic garden and arboretum. Many of the plants are labeled. Since the gardens lie near the end of the hike, if you get distracted and wander off to view plants, you are quite near the trailhead. *Note:* The trails are not named, but trail intersections are marked with a letter and number, for example, K3 or L4. With the map in this guide or an arboretum map, you will be able to easily trace your progress.

Miles and Directions

0.0 From the Wingra Springs parking lot, with your back to Arboretum Drive, take the path leaving the right-hand corner of the lot. Trace a singletrack path in hardwoods. Head left at the first intersection and begin a loop around the Indian effigy mounds. Stay right as a spur trail goes to Big Spring. Turn right at intersection K3.

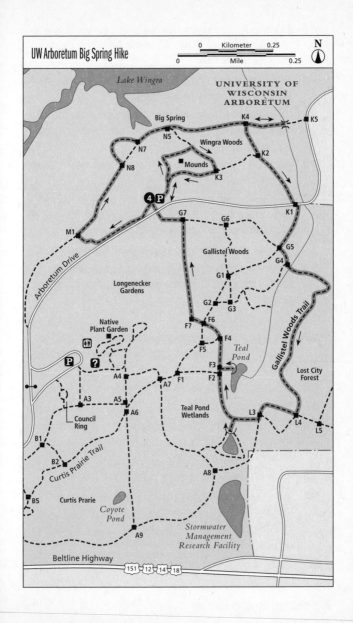

0.3 Return to the parking lot, then leave from the opposite end of the lot, hiking parallel to Arboretum Drive in pines. Note the huge trailside oak.

0.5 Reach trail intersection M1. Turn right, heading northeast in the margin between woods and marsh.

0.7 Reach trail intersection N8. Turn left and follow the marsh boardwalk. Emerge at the boardwalk at N7, then head for Big Spring.

0.8 Arrive at Big Spring, encased in stones. Keep straight, entering hemlocks.

1.0 Pass intersection K4. Keep straight to reach a boardwalk and wetland stream. Turn around at the bridge. Return to K4 and head south (left), uphill. Pass intersection K2.

1.4 Cross Arboretum Drive and enter Gallistel Woods.

1.5 Turn left at G5. Keep straight at G4 and bridge a small stream. Enter Lost City Forest and proceed through low, wet woods.

1.9 Turn right at L4.

2.0 Turn right at L3. Ahead, walk the boardwalk leading left to Pond 2. You are in the Teal Pond Wetlands, which are being restored.

2.2 Keep straight at F2. Ahead, turn right and visit Teal Pond.

2.3 Keep straight at F4.

2.4 Keep straight at F6, then turn right at F7. You are walking the margin between natural woods to your right and Longenecker Gardens to your left.

2.6 Angle left at G7. Walk parallel to Arboretum Drive.

2.7 Return to the trailhead across Arboretum Drive, completing the hike.

5 Curtis Prairie at UW Arboretum

Explore environmental history on this hike through the world's first restored prairie. Start at the University of Wisconsin Arboretum Visitor Center and skirt famed Curtis Prairie. You will then enter the Leopold Pines, named for the renowned naturalist who once worked at the University of Wisconsin. Enjoy the hardwood forest of the Noe Woods, and pass by Curtis Pond. Walk along the south edge of Curtis Prairie before nearing wetlands and returning to the arboretum visitor center, worth a visit itself.

Distance: 2.4-mile double loop
Hiking time: About 2 to 2.5 hours
Difficulty: Moderate
Trail surface: Natural surfaces
Best season: Year-round
Other trail users: None
Canine compatibility: Dogs not permitted
Fees and permits: None

Schedule: 7 a.m. to 10 p.m. daily
Maps: *UW Arboretum; USGS Madison West*
Trail contacts: University of Wisconsin Arboretum, 1207 Seminole Hwy., Madison, WI 53711; (608) 263-7888; www.uwarboretum.org

---

Finding the trailhead: From the Madison Beltline, take exit 258, Midvale Boulevard, for 0.2 mile, then turn right on Nakoma Road. Follow Nakoma Road for 0.5 mile. Turn right (south) on Seminole Highway and follow it for 0.3 mile. Turn left into the arboretum on Arboretum Drive and continue for 0.8 mile into the visitor center parking lot on your right.

Alternate directions from the east: From exit 260 on the Madison Beltline (US 12/18), take Fish Hatchery Road north for 1.1 miles to Wingra Drive. Turn left on Wingra Drive and follow it 0.6 mile to

Arboretum Drive. Turn left on Arboretum Drive and follow it 2.2 miles to the arboretum visitor center. GPS: N43 2.457' / W89 25.847'

The Hike

Nowadays, we take prairie restoration for granted. It seems to be going on at nearly all southern Wisconsin parks, whether they are city, county, or state preserves. We have realized that the prairie environment is an important component of the Midwest's greater ecosystem. And it all started here at the University of Wisconsin Arboretum. During the 1920s professors bandied about the idea of making a prairie of native plants for research and to show students and citizens what a natural prairie look like.

Simultaneously, the university was acquiring land for an arboretum. They bought a couple of farms, and from this farmland a 60-acre prairie restoration site was chosen. The spot had been planted as farmland for a century. With the help of the Civilian Conservation Corps, prairie seed was collected and planted. Other prairie seed was sprouted in nurseries and actual remaining prairie was dug up and replanted at the site. By the late 1930s, prairie flowers were coloring the landscape. Of course, there was a lot to work out as far as what restoration techniques were most effective. In 1941 John Curtis began heading the project. He introduced controlled burns to purge exotic vegetation. Mr. Curtis stayed in his position for two decades, honing prairie restoration techniques still in use today. In recognition of his service, the prairie was named for him.

Prairie restoration experimentation continues at the arboretum, and the University of Wisconsin is a leading force in this science. Of course, any ecosystem—whether it is prairie, wetlands, or woodlands—does not exist in a vacuum and is a part of a greater mosaic of intertwined flora and fauna, each needing the others to thrive. That is why restoration efforts at the arboretum are not limited to prairie. You will also see wetland restoration as well as mesic forests and oak savannas seen in southern Wisconsin. Still other areas of the arboretum include classic plant and tree collections as well as other areas replicating specific parts of the state, such as the North Woods.

On this hike you will see the prairie, hardwood forests, pines, ponds, and wetlands. The trails at the arboretum are not named. However, trail intersections are marked with a letter and number, for example C3 or A9. These numbered intersections will help keep you apprised of your whereabouts.

Miles and Directions

- **0.0** From the arboretum visitor center's main parking area look-ing south at Curtis Prairie, walk south on a mown path into Curtis Prairie. You'll reach intersection A3 shortly. Turn right here, heading westerly and soon pass a spur trail leading right to the Council Ring.

- **0.2** Stay straight as you pass intersection B1. The prairie stretches to your left, mixed with tree copses.

- **0.3** Come to intersection C1. The Curtis Lot, a popular parking area, is directly across Arboretum Drive. Keep straight, west-erly, paralleling Arboretum Drive.

- **0.4** Keep straight past intersection C3. Enter the Leopold Pines, named for Wisconsin prairie researcher and famed naturalist Aldo Leopold. Travel beneath shady pines.

- **0.5** Stay straight at intersection E5. Leave the Leopold Pines and enter Noe Woods, a hardwood forest. Curve south near the Madison Beltline.

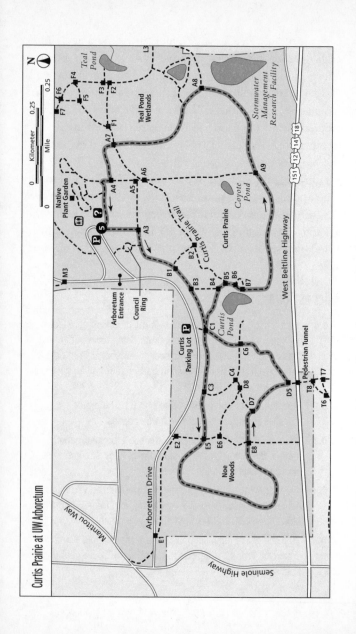

Curtis Prairie at UW Arboretum

0.9 Reach E8. Keep straight and reenter the Leopold Pines.

1.0 Turn right at D7.

1.1 Reach D5. You are very close to the Madison Beltline. A pedestrian tunnel leads right to another tract of the arboretum, but stay left here, still in the Leopold Pines.

1.2 Keep straight at C6. The trail going right dead-ends.

1.3 Return to intersection C1. Turn right here on a slender path through prairie, heading southeast. In late summer the grass will be chest high.

1.4 Reach B4. Turn right here and travel south, with Curtis Pond to your right.

1.5 Turn left (eastbound), with Curtis Prairie to your left and the Leopold Pines to your right. The nearby Beltline can be noisy, especially with a south wind.

1.8 Keep straight past A9.

2.0 Come to A8. You are near a storm-water treatment facility. Begin curving past the Teal Pond wetlands, with Curtis Prairie to your left. Pass many a tall cottonwood tree.

2.2 Keep straight at A7.

2.3 Come to A4. You are in the plant nursery area, with nearby facilities. Stay left (west) and soon pass on the south side of the visitor center.

2.4 Reach the main parking area, completing the hike.

6 New Glarus Woods Hike

This hike explores a preserved parcel of forest near the worth-a-visit town of New Glarus. Start your loop hike at a pretty picnic area, then delve into deep and regal hardwoods of walnut, oak, and basswood. The loop breaks out into colorful prairie near the headwaters of the Sugar River before turning north and rolling over more wooded hills. It then passes near a campground and over more wooded knolls before closing the loop. The hike is on state park property, which is well managed not only with regard to its natural resources but also for recreation such as hiking, picnicking, and camping.

Distance: 3.8-mile loop
Hiking time: About 2 to 2.5 hours
Difficulty: Moderate
Trail surface: Natural surface
Best seasons: Spring through fall
Other trail users: None
Canine compatibility: Leashed dogs permitted

Fees and permits: Parking pass required
Schedule: 6 a.m. to 11 p.m. daily
Maps: *New Glarus Woods State Park; USGS New Glarus*
Trail contacts: New Glarus Woods State Park, PO Box 805, New Glarus, WI 53574; (608) 527-2335; www.dnr.wi.gov

Finding the trailhead: From the intersection of WI 69 and WI 39 in the village of New Glarus, south of Madison, take WI 69 south 1.9 miles to County Road NN. Turn right on County Road NN and quickly come to the New Glarus Woods State Park entrance station. From there, drive 0.1 mile to the trailhead parking area, located on the right at the park picnic area. GPS: N42 47.220' / W89 37.865'

The Hike

New Glarus Woods State Park was named by colonists after their hometown of New Glarus, Switzerland. Though New Glarus was settled in the 1840s, the Swiss tradition remains. You can see it in the architecture of the town and in the festivals and events held there. The state park where this hike takes place is just south of New Glarus. When southern Wisconsin was being settled, people avoided the dense forest and wooded hills, opting instead for the more arable prairie, despite the fact there was a sawmill in the town of New Glarus. Don't be surprised if you see trees older than the United States while hiking here.

This hike follows the Havenridge Nature Trail throughout its length. You can get an interpretive booklet at the state park entrance station. Use numbered posts along the trail to learn a lot about these woods. The state park has been in business since 1934. It is situated on the edge of a hill and prairie and thus features habitats of both environments. Before or after your hike, enjoy a picnic at the trailhead. If time allows, you may want to camp here, at either the drive-in or walk-in campsites. The trail system connects to the town of New Glarus and the Sugar River Trail, a linear rail trail.

The forest, prairie, and hills of New Glarus Woods all add dimension to the hike. You will discover this quickly upon leaving the park picnic area. The towering, mature woods cloaking the hills have an ancient feel about them. Then suddenly you break out into prairie where colorful wildflowers and the open skies deliver a different aura. Alternate between forest and prairie, then cruise along the headwaters of the Sugar River. Cross historic County Road NN—one of Wisconsin's earliest east–west connector roads. Travelers on this road dubbed New Glarus Woods the "loneliest and wildest" part of the route. While you may not run across a bear or wolf on this hike, you may see deer and smaller critters that call this state park home.

Beyond County Road NN, the Havenridge Nature Trail rolls through more woods, then reaches a connector heading north into the town of New Glarus. Finally, it wanders the headwaters of the Little Sugar River before returning to the state park picnic area.

Miles and Directions

0.0 With your back to the park picnic shelter, cross County Road NN and pick up the Havenridge Nature Trail. Join a 4-foot-wide grassy path under tall trees. Note the tall walnut trees as you descend.

0.2 Open onto restored park prairie. Views of the grassland below and WI 69 open up to the east (left). Enjoy the flowers and berries in season.

0.4 Reenter the forest. Wander west, then south among hills.

0.6 Pop back out on the prairie. The undulating terrain allows for attractive views. Continue wandering along the nexus of forest and prairie.

0.9 Come to a trail intersection in woods. Here, the Walnut Trail leaves sharply right and shortcuts the loop. Stay straight on the Havenridge Nature Trail.

1.1 Reach the southernmost part of the loop.

1.5 Drop down off the wooded hills and enter a brushy prairie.

1.6 Cross the headwaters of the Sugar River. The trail turns right and travels upstream along the watercourse in mixed woods and savanna.

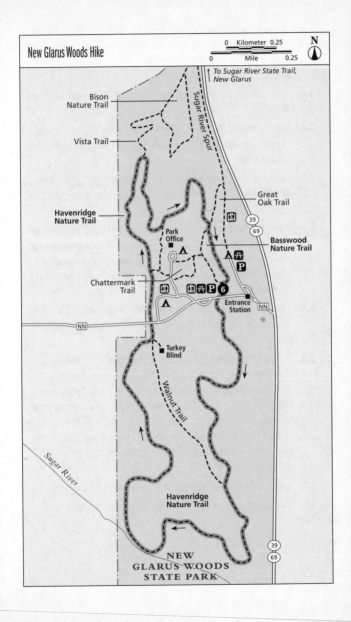

1.7 Cross back over to the north side of the Sugar River. Head north, skimming along the park boundary. Farm fields contrast with the New Glarus Woods. Continue roaming hilly forest.

2.5 Intersect the other end of the Walnut Trail. Turn left and continue north.

2.6 Reach County Road NN. Carefully cross the paved road and reenter woods, descending. The park's campground is uphill to your right.

2.9 Come to a trail intersection. A spur leads right uphill to the park's auto-accessible campground. You are now in the Little Sugar River drainage.

3.2 Meet a contemplation bench and trail intersection. Here, the Vista Trail heads north among grasses, sumacs, and smaller trees before descending into prairie and meeting up with a connector to the Sugar River Trail. This hike stays right and heads south.

3.3 Stay left at a spur leading right to the auto-accessible campground. Remain in rich woods, with their copious basswood trees.

3.6 Reach a potentially confusing intersection. First, the Great Oak Trail leaves sharply left to meet the Sugar River Spur Trail. Stay straight and go just a few feet south to another split. Here, you reach the Basswood Nature Trail. It's a loop that goes both left and right. Stay left, as the Basswood Nature Trail and Havenridge Nature Trail run together for a while on the same path. Enjoy interpretive signage while gently ascending.

3.7 A connector leads left toward the park walk-in campground.

3.8 Emerge at the park picnic area, completing the hike.

7 Donald Park Hike

Explore a portion of this 781-acre Dane County park. The refuge is centered on three trout streams—Deer Creek, Fryes Feeder, and Mount Vernon Creek—and the hills that surround them. On this hike you will head downstream along meadow-lined Deer Creek, passing a small cave before climbing into wooded hills. Enter open terrain again at Larson Pond. After completing your first loop, hike upstream along Deer Creek in an ideal mix of field, forest, and stream. Circle around an outcrop, then ascend tree-covered Hitchcock Ridge, where you pass atop a bluff and alongside rock cathedrals that present winter views.

Distance: 4.0-mile loops

Hiking time: About 2.5 to 3.5 hours

Difficulty: Moderate

Trail surface: Natural surface

Best season: Year-round

Other trail users: Equestrians on some trails

Canine compatibility: Leashed dogs allowed with county dog permit

Fees and permits: None

Schedule: Dawn to dusk daily

Maps: *Donald Park; USGS Mount Vernon*

Trail contacts: Donald Park, 1945 Highway 92, Mount Horeb, WI 53572; (608) 224-3730; www.countyofdane.com

Finding the trailhead: From the intersection of US 18/151 and County Road G in Verona, take County Road G west to Mount Vernon and WI 92. From there, turn right and follow WI 92 west for 1.7 miles to the Deer Creek entrance of Donald Park on Sutter Drive, 0.1 mile beyond the Pops Knoll picnic area entrance. Turn left on Sutter Drive and follow it 0.1 mile to the bridge over Deer Creek and a parking area on your left. GPS: N42 57.544' / W89 40.900'

The Hike

Part of the unglaciated area of Dane County, the land in Donald Park features wind- and water-carved hills and valleys. The park was formed when the county acquired two farm parcels in the Mount Vernon Creek valley. Originally settled in the 1850s by the Reverend James Donald, the land is now managed for its natural beauty. The county has an ongoing restoration process that tries to keep out invasive plants while fostering native grasses and trees. For more than 130 years, the Donald family not only had an interest in farming but also in Wisconsin politics. Today, 580 acres of the park passed through the Donald family via a combination of donated lands, purchased lands, and easements. The descendants of Reverend James Donald strongly support Donald Park, as do the Friends of Donald Park, a group active in improving the land for its natural qualities, historic preservation, and public use.

Varied environments are this hike's greatest asset. First, you will leave the Deer Creek fishing access and travel through grassy streamside ecosystems along this fast-moving, slender waterway. In summer wildflowers and high grass will border Deer Creek. As you travel downstream, trees add to the mix. Then, the stream and trail becomes pinched in by a rock bluff. Watch for a small cave. You will then leave Deer Creek near its confluence with Fryes Feeder, another trout stream. These two waterways become Mount Vernon Creek. Temporarily leave the watercourse and climb into north-facing woods of aspen, oak, and basswood. Enjoy a side trip to Larson Pond, built by an avid fisherman in the 1960s. A dock extends into the smallish tarn.

After returning to the trailhead, this hike takes you to the upper part of Deer Creek, where you eventually climb Hitchcock Ridge past a bluff and rock outcrops. Numbered intersections and maps at each trail junction make keeping up with your position on the hike easy, though the trails are not named.

Miles and Directions

0.0 Looking north toward WI 92 from the Deer Creek parking access, head right (east) downstream along Deer Creek, which will be to your left. Walk among grasses. Songbirds will serenade you here in summer.

0.3 Bridge a tributary of Deer Creek. Continue hiking in a mix of trees and meadow, bridging a second small tributary. Reach a scenic spot where Deer Creek banks up against a stone bluff. Look for a small cave above the trail. A hill rises to your right.

0.7 Reach a trail intersection. Here, a bridge leads left across Deer Creek and up the Fryes Feeder valley. Walk a few steps right, away from the bridge, and reach a doubletrack multi-use path. Turn right here, tracing the multiuse path west.

0.8 Join a narrower, hiker-only trail leading left into woods. Begin climbing up a north-facing slope. Top out, then pass near a white pine grove.

1.1 Come to a four-way trail intersection in a field. Here, keep straight on a hiker-only path toward Larson Pond.

1.2 Turn right, heading northbound after passing a spur trail leading left to the park caretaker's residence.

1.4 Keep north after crossing a doubletrack, multiuse trail. Turn into woods and come to a small stream. Hike alongside an aspen-covered hill.

1.5 Return to the Deer Creek parking access, completing your first loop. Cross Sutter Drive, then head upstream along

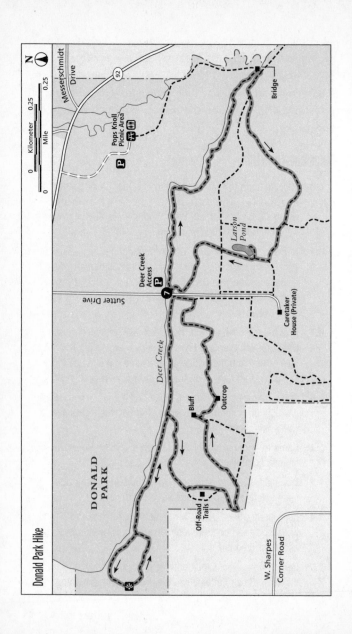

Deer Creek, with the stream to your right on a doubletrack wide grass trail. There is farmland just across Deer Creek.

2.0 Pass the path heading up Hitchcock Ridge. Keep straight along Deer Creek in mixed meadow and walnut trees.

2.2 Stay right at the loop portion of the hike, then pass a path continuing up Deer Creek. Climb a rocky hilltop.

2.6 Complete the extra loop. Backtrack to the trail leading up Hitchcock Ridge.

2.8 Turn right and begin climbing Hitchcock Ridge in fields and woods. Pass a small grassy path circling a meadow.

3.2 Top out at a four-way intersection near private property near Sharpes Corner Road. Stay left.

3.3 Stay left again, as a trail rises to a hill to your right. Cruise along margin of field and woods.

3.5 Enter woods at an intersection. Stay left and shortly come to a spur trail leading left to a perched bluff with winter views to the north. The trail along Hitchcock Ridge then descends along a castle-like rock outcrop in the woods.

3.8 Emerge at a meadow from the woods. Trace the mown path toward Deer Creek.

4.0 End your hike after heading left at a doubletrack trail within sight of the trailhead.

8 Blue Mound Loop

This hike starts at the highest point in southern Wisconsin. Soak in 360-degree views from an observation tower 1,710 feet in elevation, then join the Flint Rock Nature Trail. Circle around the north side of Blue Mound. Visit an old springhouse, then return to the top of the mound via the Indian Marker Tree Trail, winding among boulders galore. Lastly, view a tree bent in the direction of the summer solstice from the days before Wisconsin was a state.

Distance: 2.7-mile loop
Hiking time: About 1.5 to 2 hours
Difficulty: Moderate
Trail surface: Natural surface
Best season: Whenever the skies are clear
Other trail users: Bicyclists on a small part of the trail
Canine compatibility: Leashed dogs permitted

Fees and permits: Parking pass required
Schedule: 6 a.m. to 11 p.m. daily
Maps: *Blue Mound State Park; USGS Blue Mounds*
Trail contacts: Blue Mound State Park, 4350 Mounds Park Rd., Blue Mounds, WI 53517; (608) 437-5711; www.dnr.wi.gov

Finding the trailhead: From the intersection of WI 78 and US 18/151 in Mount Horeb, west of Madison, exit north to County Road ID. Turn left on County Road ID and follow it west to the town of Blue Mounds. Turn right on Blue Mounds Road. Follow it 0.8 mile, then meet Mounds Park Road. Here, stay straight and enter Blue Mound State Park. Pass the entrance station and head for the picnic area and West Observation Tower parking area. GPS: N43 1.631' / W89 51.323'

The Hike

Blue Mound has been a special place for a long time. Wisconsin aboriginals came here for ceremonial purposes as well as to hunt. Other natives thought of it as a spiritual place and enjoyed the rewarding view from its lofty location. Wisconsin became a state, citizens came to the area to mine for lead, then farm the land, and ultimately Blue Mound became a recreation destination, much as it is today. In the 1890s a horse-racing track was built atop the mound. It stretched in a half-mile oval. Interestingly, the road at the picnic area, where this hike starts, follows the route of the horse track. Later, a fellow named John Minix opened a recreation area that featured picnicking, swimming, and fishing among other activities. Blue Mound State Park includes a pool to this day, and you will hike very near it on this loop. The state park was established in 1959.

The highlights come quick on this hike. You haven't walked 50 yards from the trailhead before reaching the West Observation Tower, where views extend as far as the clarity of the sky allows. It will also give you an idea of how high Blue Mound is relative to the surrounding terrain. The hike then drops off the west side of Blue Mound, snaking among boulders. Interpretive signage adds an educational component to the hike. After meeting a spur trail to the park campground, the Flint Rock Nature Trail turns north, curving along the slope of Blue Mound. Small intermittent drainages cross the trail. The loop is extended by joining the Willow Springs Trail and the Minix Trail. Your literal low point comes about halfway into the hike, after which the route is mostly uphill. Stop by the springhouse near the park swimming pool. This area can be a bit of a maze. Join the Indian Marker Tree Trail. It travels through rocky, ferny, superlatively scenic woods before

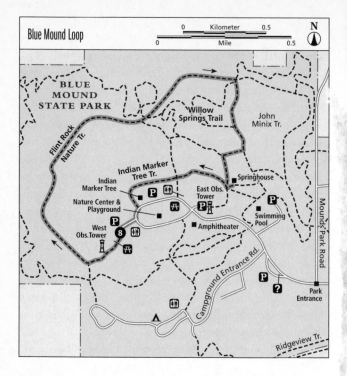

emerging near the Indian Marker Tree, where aboriginals fashioned a white oak to point toward the summer solstice sunrise. After that it is just a short walk to the picnic-area road. Once at the road the West Observation Tower parking area is within sight. Consider adding camping, bicycling, or swimming to this endeavor. In addition, the 40-mile Military Ridge State Trail passes along the south boundary of the park.

Miles and Directions

0.0 From the West Observation Tower parking area, walk west on a beaten path through grass toward the observation tower, which is within sight of the parking area. Climb the steps and soak in the views. After that, descend the tower and look for the FLINT ROCK NATURE TRAIL sign at the woods' edge. Enjoy the interpretive signage explaining the geology of Blue Mound.

0.2 A spur trail leads left to the park campground. Stay right with the Flint Rock Nature Trail. Head north in rich hardwoods.

1.1 Come to a trail intersection in woods. Here, the Flint Rock Nature Trail leaves right as a doubletrack. Head left with the doubletrack Willow Springs Trail. Ignore the singletrack mountain-biking trail, which is not shown on the map. Gently descend along the north slope of Blue Mound, crossing more drainages.

1.5 Turn right on the doubletrack Minix Trail. Ascend.

1.7 The trail leaves forest and enters brushy woods.

1.8 Reach a three-way intersection in an open area. Turn right and head gently uphill.

1.9 Come to another three-way intersection in woods. Stay left (southbound).

2.0 Come to a signed five-way intersection. Head left a short distance to see the concrete springhouse before backtracking to this intersection, then heading west on the Indian Tree Marker Trail.

2.2 Stay with the Indian Marker Tree Trail as you cross the Flint Rock Nature Trail. Continue wandering among boulders, outcrops, and ferns. Spring wildflowers are rich here.

2.6 Reach the picnic area after passing the Indian Marker Tree. You won't miss it, as the tree is signed. Walk toward the West Observation Tower parking area.

2.7 Reach the West Observation Tower parking area, ending the hike.

9 Oak Grove Trail

This hike leaves from the shoreline of a popular boating and swimming access at Yellowstone Lake State Park. Walk a wooded draw, then rise to hills above Yellowstone Lake. Here, you can gain partial views of the lake valley. The hike then traverses woods and meadows and even passes through a small gorge before returning to the trailhead. The wide, mown path and excellent trail signage make this hike a breeze.

Distance: 2.3-mile balloon loop
Hiking time: About 1.5 to 2 hours
Difficulty: Moderate
Trail surface: Natural surface
Best seasons: Spring for wildflowers; fall for colors
Other trail users: Mountain bikers for part of route; cross-country skiers
Canine compatibility: Leashed dogs permitted

Fees and permits: Parking pass required
Schedule: 6 a.m. to 11 p.m. daily
Maps: *Yellowstone Lake State Park*; *USGS Yellowstone Lake*
Trail contacts: Yellowstone Lake State Park, 8495 Lake Rd., Blanchardville, WI 53516; (608) 523-4427; www.dnr.wi.gov

Finding the trailhead: From the intersection of WI 69 and WI 39 in New Glarus, south of Madison, take WI 39 west to Blanchardville. From Blanchardville, follow County Road F west 8 miles to the state park entrance at County Road N, Lake Road. Turn left on County Road N and reach the park entrance station after 1 mile. From there, drive 0.7 mile to the trailhead parking area, located at the intersection of Lake Road and the left turn up to the state park campground. GPS: N42 46.158' / W89 58.297'

The Hike

The hiking trails are just one fine reason to visit and explore Yellowstone Lake State Park, which is centered on 450-acre Yellowstone Lake. The lake attracts swimmers, anglers, and boaters (both motor-oriented and paddlers). The campground is set up in several wooded hilly loops with ample restrooms, showers, and water spigots. I have camped here on a holiday weekend and found the outdoor spectacle to be rewarding. Most action is concentrated around the lake and not the trails. Being such an attractive lake and with so much to do, the park can get busy in summer. Spring and fall are quieter. The trails are open to cross-country skiers during wintertime. Wisconsin Department of Natural Resources property surrounds the entire lake. The state park and the trail network are concentrated on the north side of the impoundment, while the other side functions as a wildlife area.

This particular hike explores the hills and hollows draining into Yellowstone Lake. Finding the Oak Grove Trail's beginning may be the hardest part of the entire hike. You will easily spot a sign for the Oak Grove Trail near the four-way intersection of Lake Road, the campground access road, and the primary boat launch, however, you will not see a pathway entering the woods. The trail has been rerouted. Instead, the Oak Grove Trail cruises southeast, directly along Lake Road, as a grassy, mown path before turning away from the road and entering woods. The trail works deep into a hollow, then reaches the loop portion of the hike. Here, you will turn back toward Yellowstone Lake and climb a hill that rises 150 feet above the water. Wintertime views are good, but when the trees are thick with leaves, the lake is harder to see. You will then work north, crossing occasional clearings but for the most part shaded by oaks, mulberry, aspen, and other trees. Trailside blackberries and gooseberries provide tasty summertime treats. Watch for deer here too.

On your descent from the hills, you will pass through a rock-lined mini-gorge, a highlight of the trek. Before long, you are dropping back to Yellowstone Lake. Additional connections to other trails and maps at intersections make extending this hike a breeze. The Blue Ridge Trail runs the length of the park and forms a backbone to the trail network.

Miles and Directions

0.0 With the park boat ramp to your right and the access road to the park campground to your left, begin walking a mown path southeast alongside Lake Road.

0.1 Leave Lake Road and turn left (northeast) into woods, still on a mown path. A hill rises to your left and a streamlet flows to your right.

0.3 Reach the loop portion of the hike. Here, the Oak Grove Trail heads straight and acutely right. Take the leg of the Oak Grove Trail heading right. Bridge a streamlet that creates a hollow, then begin climbing a hill above Yellowstone Lake. Great oak forests rise overhead.

0.5 Rise to a point where wintertime views open of the Yellowstone Lake valley. A contemplation bench provides a place to pause. Continue a level track running roughly parallel to the lakeshore.

0.8 Turn away from the lake. Cruise north on a ridgeline in mixed woods and fields, including plenty of mulberry trees—a feast for the summertime hiker.

1.1 Pass near a stand of white pines.

1.2 Hike underneath a power line.

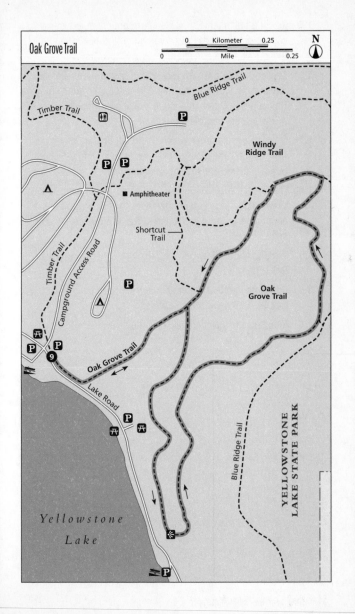

Oak Grove Trail

Kilometer
0   0.25
0   0.25
Mile

N

Blue Ridge Trail

Timber Trail

Windy
Ridge Trail

P

P   P

Amphitheater

Shortcut
Trail

Oak
Grove Trail

P

Timber Trail

Campground Access Road

P

P
9

Oak Grove Trail

Lake Road

P

P

Blue Ridge Trail

YELLOWSTONE LAKE STATE PARK

Yellowstone
Lake

P

1.3 Reach a trail intersection. Here, a short, unnamed grassy connector trail leads right a very short distance to the Blue Ridge Trail. Keep straight on the Oak Grove Trail.

1.6 Descend past oaks with widespread branches just before meeting the Windy Ridge Trail. Stay left as the Windy Ridge Trail and Oak Grove Trail run in conjunction through a mix of brush, woods, and meadows.

1.7 Come to another intersection. Head left on the Oak Grove Trail, as the Windy Ridge Trail goes straight. A forest of oak, hickory, cherry, and locust rises above.

1.8 The trail squeezes through a mini-gorge, where a creek flows to your left and a rock rampart rises to your right. Note the abundance of ferns and mosses. This is a particularly scenic area.

1.9 The Shortcut Trail leaves right. Keep straight on the Oak Grove Trail.

2.0 Complete the loop portion of the hike. Keep straight on the Oak Grove Trail, now backtracking.

2.3 Return to the trailhead, finishing the hike.

10 Yellowstone Double Loop

This hike climbs away from Yellowstone Lake, exploring different environments on two distinct loops. First, you will rise through a heavily wooded hollow, centered with a rocky drainage. The first loop takes you through woods encircling a large field, where partial views can be had. The second circuit leads you around a restored prairie, where wildflowers bloom tall in summer. Since you will be in woods, fields, and prairie, with a little luck, you may see some wildlife, from deer to songbirds to woodpeckers.

Distance: 2.5-mile double loop
Hiking time: About 1.5 to 2 hours
Difficulty: Moderate
Trail surface: Natural surface
Best seasons: Summer for prairie wildflowers; fall for colors
Other trail users: Cross-country skiers in winter
Canine compatibility: Leashed dogs permitted

Fees and permits: Parking pass required
Schedule: 6 a.m. to 11 p.m. daily
Maps: *Yellowstone Lake State Park; USGS Yellowstone Lake*
Trail contacts: Yellowstone Lake State Park, 8495 Lake Rd., Blanchardville, WI 53516; (608) 523-4427; www.dnr.wi.gov

Finding the trailhead: From the intersection of WI 69 and WI 39 in New Glarus, south of Madison, take WI 39 west to Blanchardville. From Blanchardville, follow County Road F west 8 miles to the state park entrance at County Road N, Lake Road. Turn left on County Road N and reach the Yellowstone State Park entrance station after 1 mile. From there, drive 0.1 mile to the trailhead parking area, located on the left near the first picnic area you pass on your left. GPS: N42 46.330' / W89 59.018'

The Hike

Did you know that Wisconsin has more than 8,000 lakes? The vast majority of them are natural. When glaciers swept over the Badger State, they left behind lots of places for water to gather. However, southwestern Wisconsin is part of the Driftless Area, a region untouched by the last glacial period.

The Wisconsin Department of Natural Resources decided this part of the state ought to have some lakes of its own. In the 1940s DNR personnel combed the area and picked this spot on the Yellowstone River to dam. After choosing the site, they began purchasing land from local farmers. The dam was built and the lake began filling in 1954. The DNR then stocked the lake and has done so ever since, expanding to include largemouth bass, small-mouth bass, northern pike, walleye, and panfish. Not only did they stock the lake, they also encouraged farmers in the Yellowstone River watershed to improve soil-conservation techniques to keep Yellowstone Lake from silting up. The DNR also created a waterfowl refuge in the western part of the lake. The land they purchased contains not only the lake and wetlands but also the hiking trails along hills rising above the shoreline. In addition to the hike described here, you can walk the dikes bordering the waterfowl area on the Wildlife Loop. Access to the dikes is from the park entrance station, just 0.1 mile distant from the trailhead for this hike.

Since the lake and bordering lands became public property, the DNR laid out 13 miles of trails. On this hike you will start out at a picnic shelter, with additional tree-shaded tables just across the road astride Yellowstone Lake. The Oak Ridge Trail rises behind the picnic shelter. The wide, grassy track enters a regal hardwood forest of hickory, walnut, and oak. Ferns thicken the understory. A rocky, intermittent streambed drains the hollow into which you hike. You will first make the Oak Ridge Trail circuit. It borders a field sown for wildlife and stays on the edge of the woods before traversing forest. These overlapping ecotones are places that attract turkeys and other forest critters. The woods can provide cover as you scan for deer. Stop for a partial view of Yellowstone Lake at a contemplation bench.

After completing this loop you will then hike the Prairie Loop. It traverses through and around native Wisconsin prairie, painted with a kaleidoscope of color in the summertime. Your chances of seeing wildlife increase if you make this hike in the morning or evening.

Miles and Directions

0.0 With your back to Lake Road and facing the picnic area restrooms, head right (north), passing behind the picnic shelter on a grassy track. Shortly enter forest.

0.3 Reach a trail intersection after climbing. Here, head left, staying on the Oak Ridge Trail. You will return here later.

0.4 Reach another trail intersection and keep straight, beginning the actual loop portion of the Oak Ridge Trail. Begin hiking along the edge of a large field sown with crops for wildlife, such as clover. Gain views across the wildlife meadow to the south side of the Yellowstone Lake valley. Watch as a short spur trail leads right to Ronnerude Lane.

0.9 Enter full-blown woods but continue to parallel the wildlife field. Shagbark hickories and aspens are well represented.

1.3 Complete the Oak Ridge Loop. Turn right and backtrack.

1.4 Begin the Prairie Loop on a grassy path. It soon splits. Stay left, going in a clockwise circuit. Open onto restored prairie, rising on a hill. Pass an interpretive sign that displays Wisconsin's native prairie wildflowers.

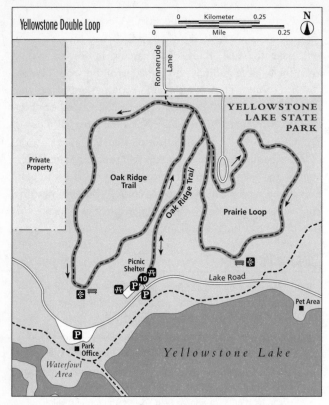

0   Kilometer   0.25

0   Mile   0.25

N

YELLOWSTONE
LAKE STATE
PARK

Ronnerude Lane

Private
Property

Oak Ridge
Trail

Oak Ridge Trail

Prairie Loop

Picnic
Shelter

10

Lake Road

Pet Area

P

Park
Office

Yellowstone Lake

Waterfowl
Area

1.5 Come very near Ronnerude Lane, an alternate access. Turn away from the prairie and enter a white pine grove. Note how the trail has been used as a fire line in managing the prairie. Look for black-scarred trunks of trees.

1.8 Pass another lake observation point, with limited views of Yellowstone Lake.

1.9 Reemerge onto the restored prairie.

2.1 Complete the Prairie Loop. Backtrack down the hollow toward Yellowstone Lake.

2.5 Return to the trailhead, ending the double circuit.

11 Pine Cliff Trail

This hiker-only path at Governor Dodge State Park packs a lot of scenery into its 2 miles. First cross a crystal-clear sandy stream, then immediately come alongside a big pine-clad bluff. The hike then climbs up the draw and circles around the top of a small wet-weather waterfall that is in the process of becoming a natural arch. You then cruise out along a ridgetop flanked on both sides by Cox Hollow Lake. The ridgeline morphs into nearly all rock and pines, and you can gain decent views of the water circling all around the peninsula. Cruise along the shoreline of Cox Hollow Lake before completing the loop.

Distance: 2.0-mile balloon loop
Hiking time: About 1 to 1.5 hours
Difficulty: Moderate
Trail surface: Natural surface
Best season: Summer for additional park activities
Other trail users: None
Canine compatibility: Leashed dogs permitted

Fees and permits: Parking pass required
Schedule: 24/7/365
Maps: *Governor Dodge State Park; USGS Pleasant Ridge*
Trail contacts: Governor Dodge State Park, 4175 State Highway 23 N., Dodgeville, WI 53533; (608) 935-2315; www.dnr.wi.gov

---

Finding the trailhead: From exit 47 on US 18/151 west of Madison, take US 18 west for 1.5 miles to WI 23. Turn right on WI 23 north and follow it into Governor Dodge State Park. Turn right just beyond the entrance station toward Cox Hollow Lake. At 1.4 miles turn right into Enee Picnic Area, on your right. GPS: N43 0.666' / W90 7.342'

The Hike

Governor Dodge State Park covers over 5,000 acres and is home to two major lakes, two campgrounds, and miles of hiking, bicycling, and horseback-riding trails. It is a large and popular park. The lakes offer a quiet setting, as only boats with electric motors are allowed. The fishing is very good, and you will be surprised at how pretty this parcel of the Badger State is. I have camped and hiked here and recommend adding other park adventures to your hiking trip here.

Upon arriving at the trailhead, you will see Enee Picnic Area, offering yet one more thing to do here at Governor Dodge State Park. A rich forest surrounds the parking area. Find the Pine Cliff Trail kiosk on the south side of the picnic area. Immediately cross a noticeably clear and sandy stream shaded by hardwoods. In just a few steps, come upon a tan cliff rising high to your right. The rock crag is cloaked in regal white pines, mosses, and ferns. Seemingly for contrast, a flat stretches to your left. Here, aquatic plants of a wetland add an ecotone to the cliff environment. The trail quickly crosses a translucent spring branch. Spring wildflowers such as Solomon seal border the singletrack path. In summer watch out for stinging nettle growing tall along the trail. During fall you will enjoy the multiple colors of sugar maples, birches, and oaks. A big hill rises to your right, and you soon climb it. The trail skirts alongside a rocky draw that will be flowing during wetter times of the year. At its height the trail curves atop an erosion-resistant cap rock. Here, you can see the layers of rock underneath the cap rock being undermined by the ceaseless drip of water, along with the cooling and warming of rock and the subsequent expansion and contraction that causes stone to break and erode. If we could only wait a few thousand more years, Governor Dodge State Park will have yet another feature: an arch.

Join a ridgeline covered with maples, white oaks, and hickory. Before long, you are making the loop portion of this hike. As you head out toward Cox Hollow Lake, the ridgeline becomes more and more narrow. The lake views open more on both sides of the ridge, even during summer when the leaves are thick. Finally, the ridgeline morphs into more rock than soil. Here, hikers can do a little scrambling and explore the various promontories stretching primarily east that offer a look to the water below. This area is a good place to relax and soak in the natural setting.

The official trail drops off the ridge and soon travels along Cox Hollow Lake. This was the first impoundment built at the state park. In 1958 Mill Creek was dammed and Cox Hollow Lake came to be. Twin Valley Lake was dammed in 1966. The park has two nice bodies of water to enjoy. Twin Valley Lake is the larger of the two, but both offer swimming, fishing, and waterside hiking. In addition, a campground is situated near both impoundments.

Continue walking along the narrowing Cox Hollow Lake. Before too long you are turning away and climbing to complete the loop, then backtracking to the trailhead.

Miles and Directions

0.0 Join the Pine Cliff Trail at the south side of the Enee Picnic Area, at a trail kiosk. Walk just a few feet, then cross an unnamed clear branch on a small bridge. Arrive alongside a pine bluff.

0.3 After climbing a hill reach a small wet-weather waterfall with an arch forming below it.

0.4 Arrive at a trail intersection. The Pine Cliff Trail goes right and straight. Stay straight toward the Pine Cliff.

0.8 Dip to a rocky gap on a narrow ridge. The official trail leaves right; however, most hikers scramble straight over the rocks to enjoy views of Cox Hollow Lake from various cliffs and

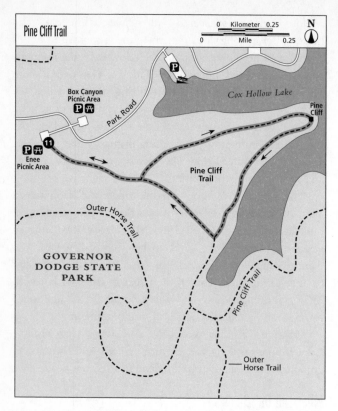

0 Kilometer 0.25

0 Mile 0.25

N

Box Canyon
Picnic Area
P ⛱

Park Road

Cox Hollow Lake

Pine
Cliff

P ⛱ 11
Enee
Picnic Area

Pine Cliff
Trail

Outer Horse Trail

GOVERNOR
DODGE STATE
PARK

Pine Cliff Trail

Outer
Horse Trail

promontories. Backtrack after scrambling and begin dipping toward Cox Hollow Lake.

1.0 Come alongside Cox Hollow Lake. Walk along the narrowing impoundment. The trail sometimes works away from the shore.

1.3 Arrive at a trail intersection. Stay right on the singletrack Pine Cliff Trail, climbing a wooded hill.

1.6 Complete the loop portion of the hike atop a ridge. Backtrack to Enee Picnic Area.

2.0 Reach Enee Picnic Area, completing the hike.

12 Stephens Falls Hike

This hike at Governor Dodge State Park has a lot to offer. How about a gorgeous waterfall, a trail cutting deep into a rock-lined gorge, views from the top of the canyon, and a visit to a historic homestead? Even though it is a little over 3 miles long, allow for plenty of time because there is so much to see! You will have lots of company at the hike's start, but after Stephens Falls, traffic drops off. You may have a little more company at hike's end, site of the Stephens Homestead, complete with lots of interesting interpretive information.

Distance: 3.1-mile loop
Hiking time: About 2.5 to 3.5 hours
Difficulty: Moderate
Trail surface: Natural surface, a little pavement
Best season: Spring or after a storm
Other trail users: None
Canine compatibility: Leashed dogs permitted
Fees and permits: Parking pass required
Schedule: 24/7/365
Maps: *Governor Dodge State Park; USGS Clyde, Pleasant Ridge*
Trail contacts: Governor Dodge State Park, 4175 State Highway 23 N., Dodgeville, WI 53533; (608) 935-2315; www.dnr.wi.gov

Finding the trailhead: From exit 47 on US 18/151 west of Madison, take US 18 west for 1.5 miles to WI 23. Turn right on WI 23 north and follow it into Governor Dodge State Park. Keep straight beyond the entrance station toward Twin Valley Lake. At 0.8 mile the Stephens Falls Trailhead is on your right. GPS: N43 1.610' / W90 7.870'

The Hike

The deservedly popular hike to Stephens Falls takes you to one of the most scenic cataracts in southern Wisconsin. The classic waterfall spills over a rock face in white ribbons, slowing in a dark pool, deep in a tree-shaded glen. The best time to go is after a storm because then the waterfall is at its highest volume. Most Governor Dodge State Park visitors make their way to Stephens Falls eventually, so the 0.2-mile walk to the falls can be crowded. The hike to the falls is dramatic as you descend into a semicircular rock amphitheater. However, there is much more to this hike. The trip down Lost Canyon is a remarkable experience. Here, sheer stone walls rise from wildflower-rich flats, forming a gorge. Immense boulders stand in repose beneath the gorge walls. The scene as a whole appears primeval. The trail crisscrosses the creek that forms Lost Canyon, allowing for multiple aquatic views. All these crossings are done using bridges. The hike leaves the gorge, then climbs to its rim. Here, you walk amid a mix of prairie and forest, skirting close enough to the gorge edge to look down where you were before, enjoying Lost Canyon from multiple perspectives.

A less popular but still worthy attraction is the preserved Alex Stephens Homestead. Though near the trailhead, it will be the last thing you see on this circuit. However, do not pass it by. The short loop goes to the location where the Stephens clan established themselves in southern Wisconsin. Interpretive signage gives in-depth explanations and insights into their day-to-day life. Stevens, a Norwegian immigrant, first built a rough cabin and developed his farm. He had multiple children who not only helped with chores but also helped him build a house later in life. You will see a display of early wagons and carriages used during this period, as well as the exact sites of farm buildings. The stone-enclosed springhouse is still intact and is likely the reason the Stephens clan located here.

Miles and Directions

0.0   Leave the Stephens Falls Trailhead on a paved path. Stephens Creek flows to your left, bordered in willows. A small prairie stretches off to your right.

0.1   Come to a four-way intersection. Here, your return route leaves left toward the Stephens Homestead. The Lost Canyon Trail leads right. Stay straight on the asphalt path toward Stephens Falls. Just ahead, a short spur trail leads to the top of Stephens Falls. Grab a limited view of the cataract. Descend on steps into a craggy rock amphitheater.

0.2   Stephens Falls forms the centerpiece of this wooded glen. Mosses and ferns grow lush under heavy tree cover. Leave the falls area and begin descending through Lost Canyon. Shortly cross over to the other side of Stephens Creek. These creek crossings are bridged. Yellow birches proliferate.

0.3   Lost Canyon closes in and Stephens Creek flows under an overhanging bluff.

0.4   Reach a three-way intersection and the end of the Stephens Falls Trail. Here, the shorter loop of the Lost Canyon Trail leaves right and uphill. Stay left, continuing down the Lost Canyon Trail.

0.5   Bridge Stephens Creek twice in succession, then arrive at a huge rock outcrop overhanging the creek, which you soon bridge again.

1.0   The canyon has widened out and you are now cruising in brushy woods on a grassy track. Cross Stephens Creek a final time. You are now on the left-hand side of the stream, heading down valley. Make a climb up the valley hill.

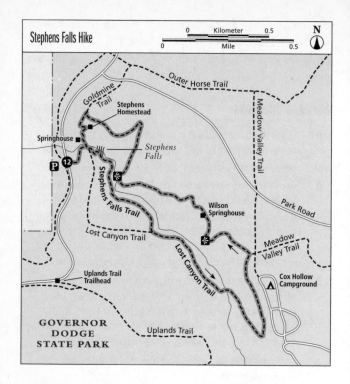

Stephens Falls Hike

0   Kilometer   0.5

0   Mile   0.5

N

Outer Horse Trail

Goldmine Trail

Stephens Homestead

Springhouse

P 12

Stephens Falls

Stephens Falls Trail

Meadow Valley Trail

Park Road

Wilson Springhouse

Lost Canyon Trail

Lost Canyon Trail

Meadow Valley Trail

Uplands Trail Trailhead

Cox Hollow Campground

GOVERNOR DODGE STATE PARK

Uplands Trail

1.2 The trail switchbacks to the north, still ascending.

1.3 Level off atop the north rim of the canyon. Short spur trails lead right to campsites at Cox Hollow Campground. Arrive alongside the canyon cliff line.

1.6 Come to a trail intersection in an open area. Here, the Meadow Valley Trail leaves right and quickly splits. Stay left on the Lost Canyon Trail, continuing in a northwesterly direction in mixed forest and meadow.

1.8 A short spur leads left to the edge of a cliff and a view below.

1.9 Another spur trail leads left to the Wilson springhouse, site of another homestead.

2.3 Pass an overlook into the heart of the canyon.

2.8 Stay left at a trail intersection, as the Goldmine Trail leaves right.

2.9 Head left into the Stephens farmstead exhibit.

3.0 Come to the springhouse and Stephens Creek; complete your loop. Backtrack.

3.1 Arrive back at the Stephens Falls Trailhead, finishing the hike.

13 Shot Tower Hike

This walk above the Wisconsin River near Spring Green—
Frank Lloyd Wright country—is rewarding through both
its human and natural history. Check out an early industry
where lead was made into rifle shot on bluffs where Mill
Creek meets the Wisconsin River. View wetlands along Mill
Creek and gain stellar views of the Wisconsin River valley.

Distance: 1.4-mile loops
Hiking time: About 1 to 1.5 hours
Difficulty: Moderate
Trail surface: Mostly natural
surface, a little asphalt
Best season: Whenever the skies
are clear
Other trail users: None
Canine compatibility: Leashed
dogs permitted

Fees and permits: Parking pass
required
Schedule: 6 a.m. to 11 p.m.
daily
Maps: *Tower Hill State Park;*
USGS Spring Green
Trail contacts: Tower Hill State
Park, 5808 C.T.H. C, Spring
Green, WI 53588; (608) 588-
2116; www.dnr.wi.gov

Finding the trailhead: From Madison, take US 14 west almost to
Spring Green. Just before crossing the Wisconsin River near Spring
Green, turn left on County Road C and follow it to soon reach the
entrance to Tower Hill State Park on your right. After entering the park
stay right, then reach the Tower Hill Picnic Area. You will see a large
parking area. The hike starts on the trail entering the woods to your
right as you are facing the picnic pavilion. GPS: N43 8.8960' / W90
2.7536'

The Hike

This hike explores the ups, downs, views, and history of a
southern Wisconsin icon. Tower Hill State Park came to be

via a mix of location, history, and chance. Lead was discovered in the Wisconsin River valley in the mid-1820s. Sometime later an entrepreneur from Green Bay named Daniel Whitney hired a fellow to build a shot tower—an operation for making musket balls from lead—near the village of Helena. The nearby Wisconsin River made transporting the shot quite convenient. The hamlet of Helena grew because of the shot tower, but when the tower went out of business in 1864, Helena faded. In 1889 Unitarian minister Jenkin Lloyd Jones bought the Helena site for $60. Jones built some cottages there before he passed away in 1918. Four years later his wife deeded the land to the state of Wisconsin for a park. Today, we have a preserved slice of beauty and history. You can hike around and below the shot tower and enjoy some other nearby activities, such as canoeing the Lower Wisconsin State Riverway, picnicking, camping, and visiting Frank Lloyd Wright's masterpiece Taliesin.

This walk first takes you from the primary park pavilion into rich woods above Mill Creek. Tower Hill State Park is located near the confluence of Mill Creek and the Wisconsin River. The bluffs and hills above the Wisconsin River were the natural features necessary to create the shot tower. It was dug by hand from the top of the bluff down through the ground to a tunnel entrance along Mill Creek. To create lead shot, molten lead needed to be dropped a long way, forming a ball and then landing in a vat of water to cool down. It was the force of gravity that allowed the lead to form into a ball.

So you will ramble through the woods, ultimately descending to the banks of Mill Creek, and see the tunnel entrance at the base of a bluff. The hike then takes you along cliffs above Mill Creek before emerging at the state park campground. From here, return near the trailhead, then walk to the top of the shot tower and visit the smelting house, where ore was melted into lead. The final part of the hike follows the Old Ox Trail, a path used by oxen to haul ore up to the shot tower. You will be heading downhill, returning to the parking area.

Miles and Directions

0.0 While facing the enclosed picnic pavilion from the large picnic area parking, look right and uphill for a natural-surface trail entering woods. Leave the picnic area and begin ascending through hardwoods.

0.2 At the intersection take the right-hand path to the east. Continue climbing to reach a gazebo atop a hill. Keep straight, descending, and soon come to an intersection. Here, a trail leads straight to the shot tower, but you will turn right, descending on a different path.

0.4 The footpath meets a park service road. Stay straight here, still descending, now on a doubletrack path. A wooded hill rises to your left. Mill Creek and a wetland stretch off to your right.

0.6 Meet a trail leading left up stairs. You will return to it. Keep straight, heading for the shot tunnel entrance where the spur ends. Here, a hole is carved into the bluff rising above you. This is where shot was retrieved after being dropped from above. The tunnel will be cool on a hot day and relatively warm on a frigid day. Note the wetlands extending toward the Wisconsin River. On your backtrack, observe all the names and initials carved into the stone bluff.

0.7 Turn right onto the trail heading up the stairs that you passed earlier. Follow Mill Creek, heading downstream, well above the waterway on a steep bluff. North-facing vistas open up.

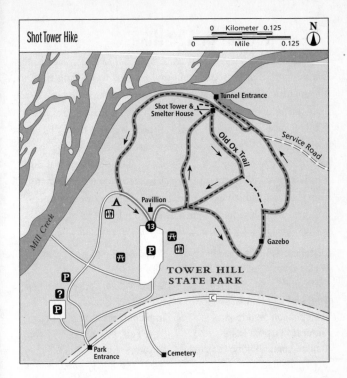

0.9 Emerge at Tower Hill campground, near campsite #13. Turn left on the campground road and follow it a short distance to the picnic pavilion. Head left up a crumbling asphalt path toward the smelting house.

1.1 Reach the smelting house after a short, steep climb. Soak in the stellar views of the Wisconsin River valley, read the interpretive info, and tour the inside of the shot tower if it is open. After exploring, leave on the Old Ox Trail.

1.2 Turn right at a three-way trail intersection. Keep descending.

1.4 Return to the trailhead near the park pavilion, completing the hike.

14 Natural Bridge Hike

This superlative Wisconsin natural feature was a long time in the making. The arch has only been within a state park for a half century, but people have been visiting it since the 1800s. Today, you can enjoy a revamped trail system that not only leads to Wisconsin's largest natural arch but also to an overlook and through the woods past an old farm building. Unlike most other areas under Wisconsin's state park system, this place is primitive as far as amenities are concerned, leaving you to focus on the natural features.

Distance: 1.3 mile balloon loop
Hiking time: About 1 to 1.5 hours
Difficulty: Easy
Trail surface: Natural surface
Best season: Year-round
Other trail users: None
Canine compatibility: Leashed dogs permitted
Fees and permits: Parking pass required

Schedule: 6 a.m. to 11 p.m. daily
Maps: *Natural Bridge State Park; USGS Black Hawk*
Trail contacts: Governor Dodge State Park, E7792 County Road C, North Freedom, WI 53951; (608) 356-8301; www.dnr.wi.gov

Finding the trailhead: From the intersection of County Road PF and US 12 near Sauk City, northwest of Madison, take US 12 west toward Baraboo for 9.1 miles to County Road C. Turn left on County Road C and follow it for 11.1 miles to the park entrance on your right. GPS: N43 20.701' / W89 55.800'

The Hike

Wisconsin aboriginals were attracted to this arch in Sauk County not only for its beauty but mainly for the south-facing rock shelter located below the natural bridge. The rock overhang located below the arch provided excellent refuge during wintertime. Native peoples used it periodically for thousands of years. Wisconsin pioneers rediscovered the bridge and began visiting it for recreational purposes in the 1870s. Word spread about this fascinating rock bridge, and visitors began carving their names onto it. In 1885 an Independence Day celebration was held at the bridge, the first recorded gathering here, but many others were to follow, especially when the introduction of the automobile increased travelers' ability to go farther faster. It became a regular on the tourist-destination list by the 1930s, and it should be on your itinerary today.

All this focus on the natural beauty attracted scientists who wanted to know more about not only big-bridge formation but also its pre-Columbian habitation. In 1957 a man named Warren Wittry of the Wisconsin Historical Society excavated the rock shelter below the natural bridge. He found evidence of fires and tool use. Some argue it is one of the oldest sites of human occupation in the upper Great Lakes region.

The arch was on the property of the Raddatz clan for generations. On your hike you will see an outbuilding left over from their day. The state of Wisconsin purchased the 500 or so acres of the natural-bridge property and it was integrated into the Wisconsin state park system. The immediate 60 acres surrounding the arch zone is an official state natural area.

The hike takes you up to the natural bridge, then to an overlook of the valley below. The hike then cruises back by the bridge and descends to the Raddatz family homesite, where you can see an old smokehouse. From there, it is but a short walk back to the trailhead. If this hike is too short,

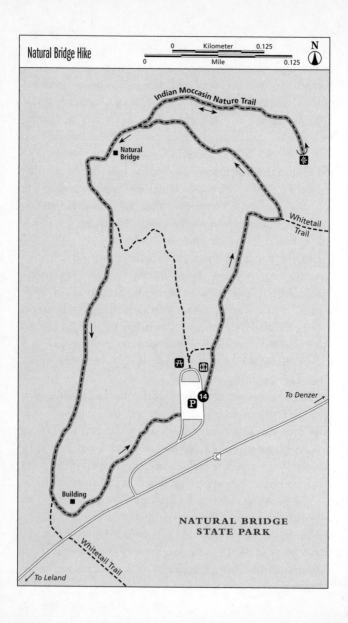

Natural Bridge Hike

Indian Moccasin Nature Trail

Natural Bridge

Whitetail Trail

To Denzer

Building

Whitetail Trail

To Leland

NATURAL BRIDGE STATE PARK

Kilometer
0   0.125
Mile
0   0.125

N

14

P

C

the Whitetail Trail makes a loop on the south side of County Road C, adding about 3 miles to your hike. It traverses primarily woods but also scattered prairie.

Miles and Directions

0.0 With your back to County Road C, take the trail leading right uphill into the woods. Another trail leads straight back from the picnic area, and your return route is to your left. Ascend on a singletrack trail uphill.

0.2 Reach a three-way intersection. Here, the Whitetail Trail leaves right to cross County Road C and loop back. Stay left and continue uphill in woods toward the Natural Bridge.

0.4 Come to another trail intersection. Turning left takes you to the Natural Bridge, right to an overlook. Turn left to see the natural bridge first. It is too tempting to see the arch first rather than the overlook. You'll soon come to the Natural Bridge. A wooden fence keeps visitors at a distance; however, you can clearly see the arch from several angles, as well as the rock shelter. From here, backtrack and head to the valley overlook.

0.6 Reach the valley overlook. Gaze over the stream valley, part of the North Branch Honey Creek watershed along which County Road C travels. A large swath of state park property rises south of County Road C. You can see the hills of the valley rising in the distance. Backtrack to the Natural Bridge.

0.8 After inspecting the Natural Bridge a second time, head south and downhill, emerging at a meadow and trail intersection. Stay right here. The trail going left heads back to the parking area. Follow an old roadbed with crumbled asphalt, the former main route to the arch.

1.2 Come to an old smokehouse very near County Road C. Turn left here and take a narrow hiking trail over a hill toward the parking area. The other end of the Whitetail Trail heads across County Road C.

1.3 Reach the parking area, completing the hike.

15 West Bluff Loop

This spectacular hike wanders atop the west bluff of Devils Lake, presenting one incredible view after another from open outcrops rising above alluring waters. The trail then descends to Devils Lake, where you walk waterside among thousands of boulders, through rock gardens, and under tall pines on the aptly named Tumbled Rocks Trail. Finally, the hike reaches the swim beach on the north shore of Devils Lake. Throngs will be sunbathing and swimming. You can join them after a short climb from the beach back to the trailhead. Be apprised that this loop is popular—solitude seekers will want to go during the week or in the morning or evening.

Distance: 2.8-mile loop
Hiking time: About 2 to 3 hours
Difficulty: More difficult due to elevation gains
Trail surface: Asphalt
Best season: Whenever the skies are clear
Other trail users: None
Canine compatibility: Leashed dogs permitted

Fees and permits: Parking pass required
Schedule: 6 a.m. to 11 p.m.
Maps: *Devils Lake State Park; USGS Baraboo*
Trail contacts: Devils Lake State Park, S5975 Park Rd., Baraboo, WI 53913; (608) 356-8301; www.dnr.wi.gov

Finding the trailhead: From Sauk City, west of Madison, take US 12 north toward Baraboo. Just before reaching Baraboo, take WI 159 east for 1.2 miles to WI 123. Turn right on WI 123 south and follow it 0.2 mile to the main north entrance of Devils Lake State Park. After entering the park at the stone columns, drive 0.4 mile to the parking area on your right. GPS: N43 25.752' / W89 44.152'

The Hike

This hike is a southern Wisconsin classic. Moreover, it is one of the best hikes in the upper Midwest. There is never a dull moment. After making the loop you will join the throngs who sing its praises. That being said, the hike can draw throngs. However, do not let that stop you. The everywhere-you-look beauty combines with postcard-gorgeous vistas. Bring your camera and allow for plenty of time, and make sure your phone is charged up to take pictures—you will be doing plenty of that.

Your hike takes you up to the West Bluff above Devils Lake. The rock atop the West Bluff, quartzite, is among the hardest rock on earth. That is why it still stands above Devils Lake—it is simply a very erosion-resistant compound. These quartzite bluffs around Devils Lake weathered less than the softer sedimentary rock that is now part of the lake bottom. Though most of Wisconsin's landscape was sculpted by glaciers, Devils Lake was not. It was formed by a combination of erosion and repeated freezing and thawing of the rock. This freezing, thawing, and resultant expansion and contraction also created the boulder fields through which you will walk.

The hike starts near the park entrance. It begins a little less than 400-foot climb to the crest of the West Bluff. Stone steps ease the ascent. Arrive at partially wooded stone bluffs. You will try to gain views and can get some partial vistas of Devils Lake below. However, you will know when the really great views open up. At one point, pass an open rock outcrop with a viewing scope to allow closer scenes of the distant hills, lake, and park facilities. Continue south along West Bluff, passing many other outcrops. They will draw you to their edges repeatedly.

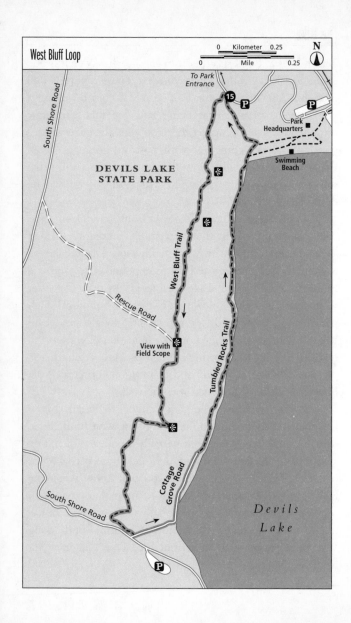

A steady descent from the line of bluffs takes you to Cottage Grove Road. The hike then passes some private cottages. Rejoin an asphalt path alongside Devils Lake. More views open as you bisect immense and incredible boulder fields. This part of the hike offers more stopping points atop some of these enormous boulders. You will come very near the action at the north shore swim beach. Then a short connector leads back up to the trailhead.

Miles and Directions

0.0 Start your hike by joining the West Bluff Trail as it heads back along the park entrance road then joins a set of ascending stone stairs. The West Bluff Trail is part of the Ice Age Trail. Views soon appear to your left among maples, oaks, and pines.

0.3 Your first clear view opens of the north-shore swim beach.

0.4 Come to a flat outcrop with more panoramas. Partial views become nearly continuous.

0.7 Reach a wide-open outcrop with a mounted viewing scope. The bluff also has an embedded USGS survey marker. But most importantly, it presents wide-open vistas from one of the highest points on the West Bluff. Note the park rescue road and phone here. The rescue road is open only to park personnel.

0.8 Come to another stellar outcrop with views to the south.

0.9 The West Bluff Trail begins descending.

1.0 A spur trail leads left to an outcrop and yet another view, with an especially rewarding panorama of the lowlands between the East Bluff and the South Bluff. The asphalt trail alternates with stone steps on the downgrade.

1.5 Emerge from the woods at the intersection of South Shore Road and Cottage Grove Road. Turn left on Cottage Grove

Road, tracing the gravel track northward. It seems like the wrong way to go, but this is the correct route.

1.6 Arrive alongside Devils Lake. Shortly pass behind some cottages, then rejoin an asphalt path, the Tumbled Rocks Trail, traveling parallel to the boulder-and-pine shoreline, along with sporadic cottonwoods.

2.0 Bisect an incredible boulder garden.

2.2 Leave the boulder garden for woods, then reemerge in another boulder garden after 0.1 mile. The large, lavender-tinted rocks make for ideal repose locales.

2.6 Reach the north shore of Devils Lake and a trail intersection. An asphalt path leaves right for the swim beach. Keep straight and then angle left for a trail entering woods, heading northwest away from Devils Lake. Climb.

2.8 Return to the trailhead, completing the hike.

16 East Bluff Loop

This hike at Devils Lake State Park has big rewards but does require some climbing. Start at the southeast corner of Devils Lake, then climb through boulder fields and rock formations to reach Balanced Rock, an unusual formation. The trail then cruises north along the edge of East Bluff, affording views of the lake, the surrounding bluffs, and toward Baraboo to the north. Drop off East Bluff, passing Elephant Cave, then come alongside a clear rocky stream. Climb through the quiet woods. Finally, backtrack down through the rock maze, enjoying more views of Devils Lake before returning to the trailhead.

Distance: 3.3-mile loop

Hiking time: About 2.5 to 3.5 hours

Difficulty: More difficult due to elevation gains

Trail surface: Asphalt, gravel

Best season: Whenever the skies are clear

Other trail users: None

Canine compatibility: Leashed dogs permitted

Fees and permits: Parking pass required

Schedule: 6 a.m. to 11 p.m. daily

Maps: *Devils Lake State Park; USGS Baraboo*

Trail contacts: Devils Lake State Park, S5975 Park Rd., Baraboo, WI 53913; (608) 356-8301; www.dnr.wi.gov

Finding the trailhead: From the intersection of County Road PF and US 12 near Sauk City, west of Madison, take US 12 north toward Baraboo for 13.5 miles to Ski Hi Road. Turn right on Ski Hi Road. Follow Ski Hi Road 1.2 miles to South Lake Road. Turn right on South Lake Road and follow it for 2 miles, passing the south shore of Devils Lake to enter the state park. Pass the entrance station and follow it to hit a T intersection. Turn right at the T intersection and soon end at a parking area. GPS: N43 24.682' / W89 43.476'

The Hike

It is 500 feet from the shoreline of Devils Lake to the top of East Bluff. And when you climb from the south shore area, you can feel every bit of it. However, you will also experience rewards every step of the way. Take your time on the initial climb—there is plenty to see. You will first leave the large picnic area on the south shore. After crossing the active railroad bed that cuts through Devils Lake State Park, you will begin twisting, turning, and angling through an incredible boulder field.

Every foot gained in height increases your panoramic view of the surrounding bluffs and waters. The immediate boulder gardens through which you walk are cool too. Just as you tire of the climb, Balanced Rock comes into view. Take many pictures and catch your breath. After reaching an intersection and leveling off, the trail will take you along the edge of East Bluff. Numerous panoramas open up, including Devils Lake below, West Bluff, and the lands to the north, including Baraboo and vicinity. Descend past the Elephant Cave, a natural rock shelter.

This temporarily ends the geological features of the hike. However, you will pass another aquatic feature, a clear rocky stream along which the East Bluff Woods Trail travels. The gravel foot bed of the East Bluff Woods Trail is a relief after the rocky steps and asphalt of the East Bluff Trail. After leaving the stream, it is a general uptick through attractive woodland exuding a sense of peace. It is certainly less crowded than other trails near Devils Lake. You will then pass a rescue road before returning to the edge of East Bluff.

Then it is one more round of winding through boulder gardens before completing the hike.

Be aware that you must ascend from the lake and climb East Bluff, then descend nearly to the bottom of the bluff before climbing yet again, then descending back to the trailhead. Allow for ample time for the elevation changes and you'll have no problem.

Miles and Directions

0.0 From the parking area, look for a sign that reads GROTTOS TRAIL, POTHOLES TRAIL, CCC TRAIL, BALANCED ROCK TRAIL. Devils Lake is in view in front of you. Begin the Balanced Rock Trail, heading north on an asphalt track that becomes gravel. Reach and carefully cross the active rail line that bisects the state park.

0.1 Reach a trail intersection. Stay left with the Balanced Rock Trail, as the Grottos Trail leaves right. An unofficial trail goes far left toward Devils Lake. Begin climbing stone steps through a hard-to-believe boulder garden.

0.2 Look for a view of Balanced Rock. To your left the flat surface of Devils Lake comes into view. Turkey vultures rise in the sky. Views improve with each step.

0.3 Arrive alongside the base of a cliff. Continue winding your way up, coming to another view of Balanced Rock. The small base of Balanced Rock connects to the top of a larger stone, giving the appearance of being two rocks, one balanced on top of another.

0.4 Reach the crest of East Bluff and a trail intersection. Here, East Bluff Trail goes left and right, while the East Bluff Woods Trail goes straight. Note the emergency call box. Head left with the East Bluff Trail, cruising north, with Devils Lake 500 feet below to your left.

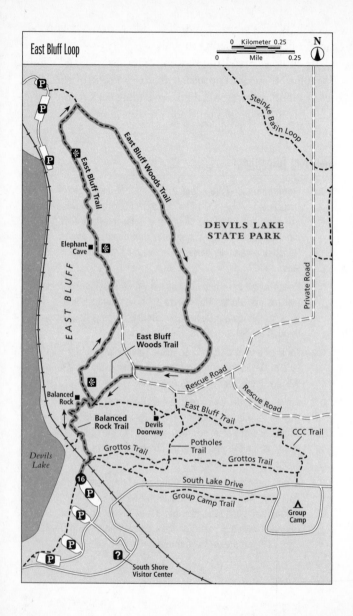

0.5 Come to a rock outcrop with views and a mounted viewing scope.

0.8 Reach a rescue road, open only to park personnel. Stay left with the asphalt East Buff Trail among pines. Be watchful for user-created trails dead-ending at outcrops.

1.1 Come back alongside the bluff rim, passing a superlative vista point. Continue descending.

1.3 Pass over the bluff, away from Devils Lake. Here, a spur trail leads right to Elephant Cave, a large opening named for a nearby rock that resembles an elephant to some. (It looks more like a buffalo to me.)

1.5 Reach a low point and trail intersection. Turn right here, joining the wide gravel track of the East Bluff Woods Trail. Soon you will come alongside a tributary of the Baraboo River. Begin a prolonged but gentle ascent.

2.4 The trail steepens.

2.7 Turn left after meeting a rescue road. Follow it, then stay right with the trail. All turns are signed.

2.9 Return to the intersection of the East Bluff Trail and the Balanced Rock Trail. Backtrack down the Balanced Rock Trail.

3.3 Complete the hike after backtracking down the Balanced Rock Trail.

17 Devils Doorway Loop

This hike may have more highlights per step than any other hike in the greater Madison area. From the south shore of Devils Lake, you will hike up through an incredible boulder garden, gaining views of the lake and surrounding bluffs with every step. You will then come to Balanced Rock, an illusionary rock formation. From there, take the East Bluff Trail away from Devils Lake, soaking in vistas galore from high rock bluffs. Take a spur to the Devils Doorway, a rockfall arch that resembles an open door suspended in midair. From there gain more views, then descend a crazy path through seemingly inhospitable rock jumbles. Level out and walk through a wooded state natural area at the base of East Bluff, gazing at the cliffs above.

Distance: 2.2-mile loop
Hiking time: About 2 to 3 hours
Difficulty: More difficult due to elevation gains
Trail surface: Asphalt
Best season: Fall or when trails are dry
Other trail users: None
Canine compatibility: Leashed dogs permitted

Fees and permits: Parking pass required
Schedule: 6 a.m. to 11 p.m. daily
Maps: *Devils Lake State Park; USGS Baraboo*
Trail contacts: Devils Lake State Park, S5975 Park Rd., Baraboo, WI 53913; (608) 356-8301; www.dnr.wi.gov

Finding the trailhead: From the intersection of County Road PF and US 12 near Sauk City, west of Madison, take US 12 north toward Baraboo for 13.5 miles to Ski Hi Road. Turn right on Ski Hi Road. Follow Ski Hi Road 1.2 miles to South Lake Road. Turn right on South Lake Road and follow it for 2 miles, passing the south shore of Devils

Lake to enter the state park. Turn left to pass the entrance station, then stay straight to quickly hit a T intersection. Turn right at the T intersection and soon end at a large parking area. GPS: N43 24.682' / W89 43.476'

The Hike

This hike is one of the many reasons why Devils Lake State Park is Wisconsin's most visited state park. Experience firsthand amazing rock formations and geological wonders. First, leave the south shore of Devils Lake, with its first-rate picnic area and swim beach. It even has a concessionaire selling ice cream and such during the warm season. In addition to this hike, you can walk a wetland boardwalk or climb the bluffs towering over Devils Lake. And this is just in the immediate trailhead area! Devils Lake State Park also presents three campgrounds for overnighting, rock-climbing and mountain-biking opportunities, and four different state natural areas within its confines. In addition, there is the lake for fishing, swimming, and boating. Only electric motors are allowed, keeping the lake quiet. And canoers and kayakers will be seen plying their boats using muscle power.

This hike offers some cliff-top walking—of course, you have to climb there from the lake. It is on the Balanced Rock Trail that you will first experience immense boulder fields in still repose, forming an inhospitable yet fascinatingly beautiful environment. The climb to East Bluff will lead you past Balanced Rock. Here, it appears a tall, narrow stone is perfectly balanced above a wider rock.

More rock formations lie ahead, the most fascinat- ing of which is the Devils Doorway. A tall rock spire has eroded and broken up, then fallen upon itself to form what looks like a doorway in the sky. It is easily my favorite rock

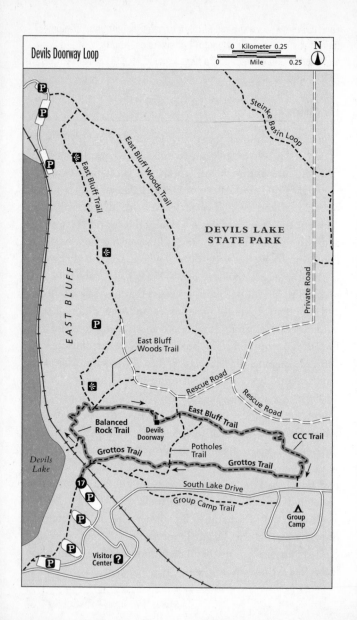

formation in the park. The CCC Trail leads down the bluff. It is a slow and challenging trip but fun too. It will seem like you're walking on air after dropping off the bluff and joining the Grottos Trail. Pass through the Devils Lake Oak Forest State Natural Area on a foot-friendly path, thus ending your hike. After undertaking this slow but rewarding trek, decide for yourself if it is the best easy day hike in greater Madison.

Miles and Directions

0.0   From the south shore parking area, look for a sign that reads GROTTOS TRAIL, POTHOLES TRAIL, CCC TRAIL, BALANCED ROCK TRAIL. Devils Lake is in view in front of you. Begin the Balanced Rock Trail, heading north on an asphalt track that becomes gravel. Reach and carefully cross the active rail line bisecting the state park.

0.1   Reach a trail intersection. Stay left with the Balanced Rock Trail, as the Grottos Trail leaves right. The Grottos Trail is your return route. A user-created trail goes far left toward Devils Lake. Begin climbing stone steps through an inhospitable yet scenic boulder garden.

0.2   Gain a view of Balanced Rock. Devils Lake becomes more visible as you ascend.

0.3   After passing through boulder fields, join the base of a cliff. The trail ascends still, then reaches a second view of Balanced Rock. The small base of Balanced Rock connects to the top of a larger stone, giving the appearance of being two rocks, one balanced on top of another.

0.4   Come to the top of East Bluff and a trail intersection. Here, East Bluff Trail goes left and right, while the East Bluff Woods Trail goes straight. Note the emergency call box. Head right with the East Bluff Trail, away from Devils Lake. Walk on rock beside cedars and wildflowers in summer in partial woods. This is a designated state natural area.

0.7 Take the spur loop leading down and to your right, leading to the Devils Doorway. View the rockfall arch and absorb still more panoramas, especially of the South Bluff.

0.8 Return to the East Bluff Trail. Keep easterly.

0.9 The Potholes Trail leads steeply to your right, cutting the loop in half. Stay on the East Bluff Trail. Pay attention as user-created trails and other paths spur off the main track.

1.0 Join the CCC Trail just after passing a rescue road to the left. Pass under a bluff then curve back east, picking your way through a geological wonderland. Be patient with your foot placement.

1.4 Reach a wooded flat and the Grottos Trail. A spur leads left to the park group camp. Turn right with the Grottos Trail, heading westerly to enter the oak forest natural area. Boulder gardens rise to your right.

1.8 Keep straight as you pass the other end of the Potholes Trail.

2.0 Pass a shortcut leading left to South Lake Road.

2.1 Stay left after meeting the Balanced Rock Trail. Backtrack across the railroad tracks.

2.2 Complete the hike after backtracking down the Balanced Rock Trail.

18 Ice Age Trail at Indian Lake Park

This hike traces the Ice Age Trail through Indian Lake County Park and around Indian Lake, an attractive tarn bordered by hill and prairie, wood, and field. First, the Ice Age Trail heads away from Indian Lake, traversing wooded hills broken by sporadic clearings. It then descends for the shores of Indian Lake, where aquatic vistas await. From there it rolls through meadows and restored prairie before crossing Halfway Prairie Creek and reaching the park boat ramp. From there, the hike joins a connector trail, skirting the north shore of Indian Lake. Complete the circuit with a short walk along the park entrance road.

Distance: 3.6-mile loop
Hiking time: About 2 to 3 hours
Difficulty: Moderate
Trail surface: Natural surface
Best season: Whenever snow is not on the ground
Other trail users: Skiers when snow is on the ground
Canine compatibility: Leashed dogs allowed with county dog permit

Fees and permits: None
Schedule: 24/7/365
Maps: *Indian Lake Park; USGS Springfield Corners, Black Earth*
Trail contacts: Indian Lake Park, 8183 Highway 19, Cross Plains, WI 53528; (608) 224-3730; www.countyofdane.com

Finding the trailhead: From the intersection of US 12 and US 14 in Middleton, west of Madison, take US 12 west for 10 miles to WI 19. Turn left and follow WI 19 west for 2 miles to the entrance to Indian Lake County Park. Follow the entrance road to the dead end into the main parking lot for the park. GPS: N43 11.371' / W89 37.280'

The Hike

This Dane County Park hosts a portion of the Ice Age Trail. Indian Lake County Park covers nearly 500 acres in northwestern Dane County. It is an important link in the Ice Age Trail corridor in Dane County. A spider web of trails runs through Indian Lake Park, especially on the south side of Indian Lake. Most of these trails are used during the winter as cross-country ski trails. Yet another mini-network of trails wanders through a prairie and is primarily used by dogs and their owners. Still other trails are used by snowmobilers in the winter. The best way to execute a successful and rewarding hike at Indian Lake Park is to simply follow the Ice Age Trail through the park, then use a connector path to make a loop. Otherwise, the sheer number of trail intersections and ski paths could drive a hiker crazy. Just follow the yellow blazes of the Ice Age Trail and you will be fine. *Note:* At times the Ice Age Trail will go against the direction of ski trails, and you will be hiking toward WRONG WAY signs. Ignore these signs as they are for skiers only and do not apply to hikers. Also, remember that hikers are not allowed on trails when snow is on the ground.

This portion of the Ice Age Trail cruises along and near Indian Lake, a shallow depression formed by an enormous block of melting ice during the last glaciation. The Ice Age Trail is one of Wisconsin's finest outdoor assets. It is one of the eleven national scenic trails in the United States. The idea of a path extending the length of the terminal moraine of the Badger State's last glaciation was hatched in the 1950s. Ray Zillmer not only thought up the idea but also founded the Ice Age Park and Trail Foundation, the forerunner to today's Ice Age Trail Alliance, the group charged with maintaining and extending Wisconsin's master path. In addition to this Ice Age Trail hike, consider taking the short walk up to the hilltop chapel at the park. It was built in 1857. The chapel access trail leaves east from the main parking lot.

Miles and Directions

0.0   Leave south through an archway from the primary parking lot. Look for the yellow blaze denoting the Ice Age Trail. Ski trails quickly spur right. Much of the Ice Age Trail also traces winter ski trails.

0.1   Pass around a gate atop a small hill. Stay with the double-track trail. Always find the yellow blazes of the Ice Age Trail.

0.2   Pass ski trails, grassy in summer, and approach the hilltop skier-warming house.

0.4   Pass through an aspen grove set amid small prairies.

0.5   The Ice Age Trail turns right, heading westerly.

0.8   The Ice Age Trail turns right and downhill, toward Indian Lake. Pass through hardwoods of maple, oak, aspen, and basswood.

1.2   Level off and Indian Lake comes into view. A spur trails lead right back toward the parking area. Stay west, traveling parallel to the lakeshore.

1.6   The Ice Age Trail leaves the lake while another trail continues along Indian Lake. Ascend from the water amid prairie and walnut trees.

1.7   Top a hill and turn right. Views open of grassland below.

1.9   Top out on another hill with more views. You are near the stone farmhouse of the property. Descend north, passing dog trails leading right.

2.0   Bridge the outflow of Indian Lake, Halfway Prairie Creek. Turn right, heading east. Arrive at the lakeshore.

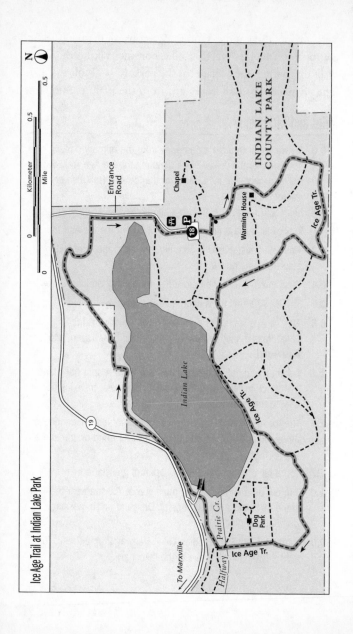

Ice Age Trail at Indian Lake Park

2.4 Cross the boat ramp entrance road. Leave the Ice Age Trail. Keep straight on an unnamed connector trail and cruise along the north shore of Indian Lake. The trail and WI 19 run close together. Pass occasional lake accesses.

3.0 The road and trail separate. You will approach farmland, then trundle along a willow marsh.

3.4 Reach the park entrance road. Turn right here, following the road toward the parking area.

3.6 End the hike at the parking area after passing below the park picnic shelter.

19 Table Bluff

This Ice Age Trail segment is rewarding enough to do as a out-and-back hike, even though you can use a shuttle as an end-to-end trek. Leave Table Bluff Road and Table Bluff itself, then follow a singletrack path through hills rolling above a tributary of Black Earth Creek. The path traverses oak savannas, then dips to cross a streambed. Reenter woods and cruise an impressive ridgeline southward that culminates in a view of ponds, grasslands, farms, and woods of southern Wisconsin. Much of the terrain has been restored to its pre-Columbian state, from the prairies to the oaks.

Distance: 4.4 miles out and back

Hiking time: About 2 to 3 hours

Difficulty: Moderate

Trail surface: Natural surface

Best season: Year-round

Other trail users: None

Canine compatibility: Leashed dogs allowed

Fees and permits: None

Schedule: 24/7/365

Maps: *Ice Age Trail—Table Bluff Segment; USGS Black Earth, Cross Plains*

Trail contacts: Ice Age Trail Alliance, 2110 Main St., Cross Plains, WI 53528; (800) 227-0046; www.iceagetrail.org

Finding the trailhead: From the intersection of County Road P and US 14 in Cross Plains, west of Madison, continue west on US 14 for 1.3 miles to County Road KP (County Road KP comes just after bridging Black Earth Creek on US 14). Turn right on KP and follow it 2.4 miles to Table Bluff Road. Turn left on Table Bluff Road and follow it 0.2 mile to the trailhead on your left. GPS: N43 8.626' / W89 40.220'

The Hike

This segment of the Ice Age Trail travels through a part of the state unaffected by glaciers, the so-called Driftless Area. However, just because it was not glacier-carved does not mean it is not worth hiking. The trail alternates between ridges rising 200 feet above a vein-like network of tributaries feeding Black Earth Creek. It also alternates between southern hardwood forests, oak savannas, and "goat prairies," the name given to native grasslands located on steeply sloped terrain, seemingly only suitable for goats. Part of the land this hike travels is owned by the Ice Age Trail Alliance and another portion uses private property. Both tracts are using fire, mowing, and herbicide spraying to restore native vegetation. The results are paying off, and you will get to see some of the most northerly examples of the pale-purple coneflower in Wisconsin, along with a host of other prairie wildflowers. You will also gain views through the oak savannas, where the density of trees is light.

To access the south end of this hike, making it an end-to-end venture, leave US 14 west of Cross Plains and turn right onto County Road KP. Follow it for 0.3 mile, then turn left on Scheele Road. Follow Scheele Road for 0.3 mile and you will see a right turn for Ice Age Trail parking. However, please do not park your vehicle long-term as there is limited parking along the road. The parking area at Table Bluff Road is better suited for parking. A pair of white-blazed spur trails adds to the potential trail mileage in the event you are not interested in backtracking along the official Ice Age Trail.

After leaving Table Bluff Road, where the actual Table Bluff stands west of the trailhead, the Ice Age Trail weaves south through a mix of forest and meadow on a singletrack

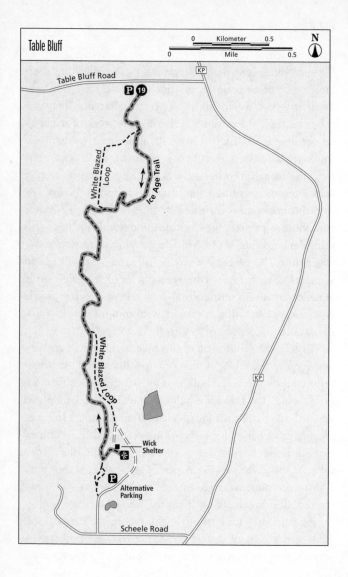

path. The hilly terrain allows for views. Watch for the large trailside oak tree. The trail then passes through a restored oak savanna before dipping into a tributary of Black Earth Creek. You get a far-reaching view to the south in this grassy valley flanked by hilly ridges. Work your way south along a linear ridgeline that culminates at a south-facing goat prairie. Here, the ridge ends and slopes away, opening up views of pothole ponds and grasses, framed in farmland and tree-clad hills. This view is the payoff. You can see the end of this Ice Age Trail segment below, but I recommend backtracking or using the two white-blazed spur trails rather than going end to end.

Miles and Directions

0.0 Leave the gravel parking area on Table Bluff Road and head south on the Ice Age Trail among woods and meadow.

0.2 Dip off the hillside and pass a massive oak. Here, a white-blazed spur trail leaves right and reconnects to the Ice Age Trail after a half mile. Wander through oaks and prairie.

0.8 After crossing an intermittent streambed, the Ice Age Trail meets the white-blazed spur. Keep straight on the Ice Age Trail. Leave the Ice Age Trail Alliance property and enter Swamplovers property. Climb alongside a wooded ridge, heading south, still on a singletrack trail.

1.2 Cross a bridge over a stream branch. Keep southerly in woods.

1.5 A second white-blazed spur leaves the Ice Age Trail. It also travels south and meets the Ice Age Trail at a picnic shelter. Keep south in oaks and aspens on the Ice Age Trail. Watch for occasional rock outcrops.

2.1 Reach a trail intersection after passing through an oak savanna. Here, a spur trail leads left up to a shelter and viewpoint with interpretive information. This is also where the second white-blazed spur trail reunites with the Ice Age Trail. Follow the spur trail to the shelter and interpretive viewpoint.

2.2 Arrive at the prairie viewpoint, which offers interpretive information. Soak in the views, then backtrack or join the white-blazed spur northbound, passing the nearby shelter. It is also 0.2 mile down to the Scheele Road trailhead.

4.4 If backtracking on the Ice Age Trail, reach the Table Bluff Road trailhead.

20 Governor Nelson Circuit

This hike travels the gentle hills, green forests, and open prairie landscapes of Governor Nelson State Park, situated on the northwest shore of Lake Mendota. The hike is a reflection of the greater Madison–Indian history of Panther Mound, regal oaks, and restored prairies with extensive views of neighboring farms and forests, all within proximity of a scenic body of water.

Distance: 2.0-mile loop
Hiking time: About 1 to 2 hours
Difficulty: Easy
Trail surface: Natural surfaces
Best season: When snow is not on the ground
Other trail users: None
Canine compatibility: Leashed dogs permitted
Fees and permits: Parking pass required

Schedule: 6 a.m. to 11 p.m. daily
Maps: *Governor Nelson State Park* summer-use map; *USGS Waunakee, Madison West*
Trail contacts: Governor Nelson State Park, 5140 County Hwy. M, Waunakee, WI 53597; (608) 831-3005; www.dnr.wi.gov

Finding the trailhead: From Madison, join WI 113 north and take it to County Road M. Head west on County Road M and follow it for 2.6 miles to reach the park entrance at Oncken Road. Turn left, entering the park, and follow the main park road to the boat landing and fish-cleaning-station area. From the boat ramp, walk back down the access road a short distance and pick up the Woodland Trail. GPS: N43 7.791' / W89 26.091'

The Hike

Set on the northwestern shore of Lake Mendota, Governor Nelson State Park provides a relatively large network of hiking trails within its smallish confines. The park is perhaps best known for its swimming opportunities at Indianola Beach. However, state park personnel have been hard at work restoring the landscape to its pre-Columbian state, reestablishing the prairies, marshes, and oak savannas that once covered southern Wisconsin. Unlike most state parks, camping is not allowed, but in addition to hiking, visitors can picnic, visit the beach, and launch their boat from the ramp near the starting point of this hike. There is also a pier for shore anglers.

The trails are used for hiking during spring, summer, and fall. However, during winter when the trails are covered with snow, hiking is not allowed. The groomed paths of the state park are popular with cross-country skiers during that time. This particular hike covers but 2 miles of the larger trail system. A look at the summer-use map for the state park will give you more ideas for hiking. The state park is known for its wildflowers, both in the prairies during summer and woodlands in spring.

You will pass the Panther Mound on your hike. Mound-building aboriginals were active on the shores of Madison-area lakes. Panther Mound is suspected to have been built between AD 500 and 1600. The long mound stretches for nearly 360 feet in length. It is still intact. A spur trail on this hike curves by the mound. Sometimes it is hard to visualize what you are seeing because they are so long and low and have been subjected to the ravages of time. It is not clear whether these mounds were built for burial purposes, for ceremonial or religious purposes, or to simply honor a group of people or animals such as the panther. However, most of the effigy mounds resemble animals such as deer, bears, and turtles. Beyond the Panther Mound you will also come across a set of six conical mounds set in a row.

Starting your hike near the boat launch, take a minute to walk out there and grab a view of the state capitol across the lake. You then join the Woodland Trail, heading south to come along the aforementioned Panther Mound. The second set of mounds, the conical ones, come next. After leaving the hardwoods, you will enter into prairie where native grasses and hills combine for good vistas. Return to the woods before completing the loop hike.

Miles and Directions

0.0 From the park access road near the boat landing, walk back toward the park entrance a short distance, then pick up the Woodland Trail. Travel westerly, roughly paralleling the park access road.

0.1 Come to a trail kiosk and alternate trail access. Keep straight on the Woodland Trail.

0.2 Reach a trail intersection and the loop portion of the Woodland Trail. Stay left (southbound), entering an oak savanna.

0.4 Reach the spur loop at the Panther Mound. Stay left, circling by the earthen mound.

0.5 Return to the Woodland Trail.

0.6 Top out on a low hill, reaching the conical mounds. Arrive near private property toward the lake.

0.8 Reach a trail intersection. Here, a spur trail leads left to some little-used park facilities. Stay right with the Woodland Trail as it turns west, then north. Roll over some low wooded hills.

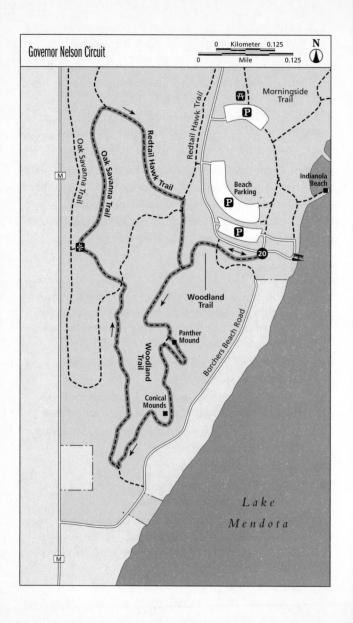

Governor Nelson Circuit

1.1 Reach a four-way intersection. Here, benches overlook a little prairie to the east. Here, turn left (not acutely left), joining the Oak Savanna Trail. It travels mostly prairie as a mown path.

1.2 Reach a scenic overlook with views to the west and north atop a small hill. A mown path leads left to the portion of the Oak Savanna Trail astride County Road M. Keep straight on the Oak Savanna Trail. Stay in the prairie.

1.4 Pass the first of two short mown paths leading right, short-cutting to the Redtail Hawk Trail.

1.5 Meet the Redtail Hawk Trail. Turn right here, heading southeast through prairie.

1.8 Come to a two-way intersection. Stay right and quickly come to another trail intersection. Stay left here, heading clockwise on the Woodland Trail.

1.9 Complete the loop portion of the hike. Backtrack on the Woodland Trail, passing by the trail kiosk a second time.

2.0 Return to the trailhead near the park boat ramp, completing the hike.

About the Author

Johnny Molloy is an outdoors writer based in Tennessee. He has averaged more than 100 nights in the wild per year since the early 1980s, backpacking and canoe camping throughout the country, in nearly every state. His efforts have resulted in more than fifty books, including hiking guides to Virginia, West Virginia, and Tennessee, as well as tent-camping guides to Colorado, Wisconsin, Tennessee, the Carolinas, Georgia, and the Smokies. He continues to write and travel extensively to all four corners of the United States, partaking in a variety of outdoor endeavors. For the latest on Molloy, visit johnnymolloy.com.

A partial list of Molloy's FalconGuides includes:

A FalconGuide to Mammoth Cave National Park

Best Easy Day Hikes Cincinnati

Best Easy Day Hikes Greensboro and Winston-Salem

Best Easy Day Hikes Jacksonville, Florida

Best Easy Day Hikes New River Gorge

Best Easy Day Hikes Richmond, Virginia

Best Easy Day Hikes Springfield, Illinois

Best Easy Day Hikes Tallahassee

Best Easy Day Hikes Tampa Bay

Best Hikes Near Cincinnati

Best Hikes Near Columbus